George Linley

The Modern Hudibras

A Poem in Three Cantos

George Linley

The Modern Hudibras
A Poem in Three Cantos

ISBN/EAN: 9783744713115

Printed in Europe, USA, Canada, Australia, Japan

Cover: Foto ©Thomas Meinert / pixelio.de

More available books at **www.hansebooks.com**

SECOND EDITION—ENLARGED.

THE

MODERN HUDIBRAS;

A Poem,

IN THREE CANTOS;

BY

GEORGE LINLEY,

AUTHOR OF MUSICAL CYNICS OF LONDON.

LONDON:

JOHN CAMDEN HOTTEN, 151, PICCADILLY.

1864.

THE

MODERN HUDIBRAS.

CANTO I.

1.

'Tis morning tide, the wind blows fresh and keen
From off that sea where ship is never seen.
'Tis not the season; dull as dull can be
Looks that starv'd, straggling town without a tree.
If George, the Prince of *Whales*, no fabled triton,
Had never set his royal feet in Brighton,
The wretched place, fit but for London jugglers,
Had been a nursery for tars or smugglers,
And not, as now, a hive for used-up drones,
Far-seeing widows, fast young maids, and crones;
Had Nash that foul pavilion never framed,
The spot had been unknown, untrod, unnamed.

2.

Upon the beach a lonely figure stood,
That seem'd, the while, in calculating mood;
Anon he paced along the shingled shore,
His speed increasing as he walked the more;
One hand went up, the other down, like sails
Of wind-mill working when the breeze prevails;
And then, as if unto the waves he'd shout,
Like some poor ranting player, strut about,
In eloquence a very water-spout,
So torrent-like flowed ev'ry thought and word.
It must have been a treat, could one have heard
The orator express his wants and wishes,
Which only Neptune *could* hear, or the fishes.

3.

What looks he for? what doth he fear or hope?
His hands are rais'd; they bear a telescope:
Some object, hidden to the naked eyes,
The sea-side watcher through his glass descries.
Great Galileo's name with reverence mention,
Thank we his shade for this improved invention.
Sailors! who plough the dark and restless deep,
Tourists! who love at all to take a peep,
Betters and Black-legs! who frequent the races,
Dandies and Doxies! in your opera places,
Loungers on Land! fair Syrens by the Sea! O!
Pledge, when the glass goes round, great Galileo!

4.

Nearer and nearer still that object seems,
The gazer's brain with speculation teems;

No tiny mast, nor canvass spread, denotes
That it belongs to any class of boats;
'Tis not a grampus, nor a turtle rare,
That tow'rd the strand those ocean-waters bear:
What is it, driving on to shore so fast,
Propell'd as by some hidden, noiseless blast?
Within a cable's length the monster comes,
The glass is lower'd, the wand'rer twirls his thumbs,
As, from the small, trim craft, now plainly seen,
A stranger stept, in suit of bottle-green.

5.

.“ Friend!” quoth the new arrival, with a wink,
“ We must have met before to-day, I think.”
Our ancient Comrade simply gave denial,
And did not bandy words as on a trial;
He but affirm'd—'twas odd he never swore
He had not seen the gentleman before:
Then added, with a sort of shrug, half boast,
'Twas his first visit to the Sussex coast;
That, as he strolled along and watch'd the tide,
He saw a something on the waters ride,
And waited anxiously, with glass in hand,
Till that mysterious something neared to land.

6.

“ And well and opportunely, John, I came.
Nay, start not that I call you by your name;
Though not so trim in garb, you are the same:
So come along with me in my boat-car;
'Tis made to sail, or mount to yonder star;

With novel gas, unknown to earth, I'll puff it;
Its giant strength will ev'ry current buffet.
Behold! these tubes are wing-like; we can soar
To heights unreach'd by Aeronauts of yore;
Traverse at such a speed through th' ambient air,
That railway train directors e'en would stare;
Smooth as a bird, through realms of space we'll swim,
Without the risk of breaking neck or limb."

7.

"Mount! mount! I'm ready; trust to my balloon
For reaching London ere the glow of noon.
Who thy Companion is seek not to know;
Enough that I am great, above, below;
But there is not a Sinner, nor a Shaker,
That would not laugh to see John B. the Quaker
Taking an early summer-morning ride,
With his Satanic Majesty for guide.
I have been sorely scandalized for years
By some who figure in the House of Peers;
When you descend, please tell the Earl of Wilton
No one has done me justice but John Milton."

8.

Halting where lately stood a horse bazaar,
The travellers saw, beneath their magic car,
A monster tabernacle in reversion,
Wherein is preached the doctrine of immersion;
There white-robed Virgins of the middle rank
Stand waiting for their turn beside the tank;
The cautious preacher for the worst prepares,
Jerkin and boots of India rubber wears.

He's guarded thus from ague or the cramp,
While doing duty in that dismal swamp:
He lands—he shivers—drips from top to toe—
Looks not unlike a half-drown'd Esquimaux.

9.

The reverend Mime, to illustrate his tale
How souls reach hell, slides down the pulpit rail;
The act and word, adroitly thus combined,
Conviction carry to the sinner's mind.
The cunning Mountebank, with knowing look,
Smiles blandly as he thumps the holy book,
And breathes damnation to his sleek-faced crew,
For all the pence he from their pockets drew.
The Stage and Pulpit, both alike defaced,
Now pander to a vile sensation taste,
Forsake the paths that Wit and Virtue trod,
And desecrate the laws of Nature and of God.

10.

We'll draw a contrast to this water-cure;
All have their foolish vanities, be sure!
The veriest knave that chuckles in his sleeve,
While cheating those who in his faith believe,
Contrives to throw an air of truth about him,
That none but Sceptics have the heart to doubt him.
He guides his flock as by some hand unseen,
Leading them on through pastures fair and green,
Till he secures their consciences and pelf:
In their debasement glorifies himself.

11.

The bells give warning for the hour of pray'r,
When rigid formalists to church repair;
The poor Plebeian o'er the gutter strides,
While in his gilded coach the Prelate rides;
That modest monarch of a good, fat See,
Unknown upon the shores of Galilee;
Unlike the ancient, barefooted Apostles,
To pomp and power the modern Bishop jostles;
Declaims in senates, rules with iron rod
The fawning sycophants who court his nod;
Denounces, as heretical and base,
All plans to socialize the human race,
To ease the fetters that enslave mankind,
To break the film that so enshrouds the mind.
Rome, in her darkest history, never saw
A truer tyrant than the one we draw.

12.

Behold yon ambling female Parvenu,
In ample garniture of brightest blue!
A bonnet, towering o'er false, sandy locks,
Conceals a neck that all description mocks.
With lusty calves and long gold-headed cane,
And prayer-book borne in Pharisaic vein,
A tall, broad-shoulder'd flunky, on tip-toes,
Bouquet in bosom, and black patch on nose,
His model mistress follows to the door,
Then bows, and yields the massive book he bore.

13.

A solemn strain peals through the sacred aisle,
The Dean and Curates entry make the while.
" Rend not your garments ! " with a modest breath,
A pale youth simpers to those souls beneath.
" Contract your garments ! " had he power to say,
Methinks commotion would the sex display.
At church, at court, at comedy, one groans,
Opprest with weight of steel, of hoops, of bones.
Preaching and prayers, alas ! are fruitless, vain ;
Poor Nature ne'er will be herself again !

14.

Accursèd fashion ! that for ever strives
To hold in leading-strings maids, widows, wives !
Some titled Beldam, or some foreign Madam,
Has set the mode e'er since the fall of Adam ;
The vice of dress, extravagance, and pride,
Is universal—spreads contagion wide :
The Peasant Girl, no more in russet guise,
The Peeress now in round-about outvies.
Swell'd out, puff'd up, like bladder blown by wind,
What pleasure can a handsome woman find
To thus deform herself to human sight ?
Inspire disgust where she should yield delight ?
To those, ill-favored both in shape and size,
Leave such inventions—Nature Art defies.
To sweep the streets with silk is downright evil ;
Waste is a crime detested by the Devil ;
Whose knowledge, whate'er else he may possess,
Entitles him to say a word on dress.

" There *is* a secret, John, you may depend
On this," quoth Hudibras unto his friend,
" Which you, so modest, never would suspect :
The reason, then, is, *why* they are so deckt,
That Dames, if not to Virtue's laws exact,
May hide 'neath Crinoline the damning fact."

15.

To ride a horse one has no need to flog,
To journey any where one likes incog.
To feel that full and perfect liberty
Which only springs from knowing one is free,
At least is pleasant, whate'er others say,
Who think the charm of life is in display.
Some power in locomotion surely lies,
That bids the spirits to the highest rise;
The rail-road whistle and the boatman's song
Are not unwelcome as we speed along;
But travellers ne'er will find a land of honey,
If they are poorly, or be short of money.

16.

O'er the Dilkoosha Palace of Delight,
Whose domes were costly, though not water-tight,
They hover in their marvellous machine,
Observing all things, yet by all unseen :
John, twisting round the watch-chain in his fob,
Cried, " I have witness'd, shared in many a job,
But I affirm, by Shuttle, Loom, and Spindle,
This is, of all, the most gigantic swindle."

17.

The Exhibition Lords of Sixty-two,
Acting as *very clever people* do,
Find now, alas! their pet, their royal scheme,
Is but the baseless fabric of a dream.
'Tween Architect and Builders, it appears
They'll get a tott'ring house about their ears.
The vaunted pile, the wonder of all wonders,
Has proved from first to last a chain of blunders.
The Commons spurned the undigested heap,
Though interested parties swore 'twas cheap;
John Bull, for once, in this affair was lucky;
To vote against a Court Cabal was plucky.
Invest the money, if you like, in cotton;
But not in leaky roofs, nor floorings rotten."

18.

Who will forget the pompous, grand display
That open'd up that monster of the day?
With Royal Princes, London Cits and Factors,
Provincial Mayors, and Railway Contractors,
Archbishops, Authors, Artists, Sculptors, Peers,
M.P.s, C.B.s, and Civil Engineers,
And pious Parsons, thrown in with a grace,
To balance others somewhat out of place;
This Omnium Gatherum leaves old Noah behind,
With all his twos and twos, each of their kind.

19.

Who the prime puppet of the show forgets,
The flaming Marshal of the Marionnettes,

Equipt in gorgeous military garb,
Foaming and fretting like some fiery Barb;
Restless as Ocean, ev'ry body tiring,
Vap'ring, gesticulating, and perspiring?
He *did* look hot—excreted a good deal;
It might be over-fat, or over-zeal;
But as he wiped his brow with his white silk,
A press-reporter cried, "that's Wentworth Dilke!
The new-made Baron of that Ilk—I mean
The Athenæum and Horticultural Magazine."

20.

Who, too, forgets the Nave and its approaches,
Choked up with Pickle trophies and Stage-coaches?
While upside down the Italian Court was turn'd,
And works of art lay quietly inurn'd?
Who can forget the Catalogue of Strictures
Publish'd about the Sculpture and the Pictures,
The authorized edition on the spot,
That perish'd, like our ships, of the dry rot?
And then the dear Veillard-Cadogan dinner,
Which, after eating, seemed to make you thinner;
'Twas an outrageous mockery and a mummery,
Which, in familiar phrase, the Cooks call flummery.
May none e'er look upon the like again!
'Mortibus est!' groan'd Hudibras; John cried 'Amen!'

21.

Steering west centre by the Postal Guide,
The Foundling Hospital our travellers 'spied.
"Ah me!" quoth Hudibras, "these English *preach*,
But do not always *practice* what they teach:

Their Gallic neighbours Infidels they call,
And hint they no religion have at all;
But these said Infidels, if such they be,
Have sense at least in their philosophy;
Against existing miseries provide,
Look danger in the face, and stem the tide;
For poison in our natnre, skill may bring
An antidote to take away the sting.

22.

" 'Twas such a spirit Captain Coram show'd,
When he the Foundling Hospital endow'd.
The seaman knew that boys and girls were born,
Whose hapless mothers would be held in scorn,
If, friendless, houseless, they were left to roam,
Without a father's love, without a home.
Peace to his manes! Though the Founder's dead,
Still Propagation lives; the Vice has spread;
But no increase of means the Powers afford
To fallen sinners needing bed and board.
There have been slanders spoken, and conjectures,
Attaching blame to the Trustees—Directors.
The right belonging to these stray-born elves,
Some people say, they keep unto themselves;
And though the Law forbids them to abuse it,
They *have* a privilege—and fail not to use it.

23.

" In Paris, there's a street, the 'Rue d' Enfèr,'
O'er which I watch," said Hudibras, " with care;
The feudal Lord am I; the Sovereignty,
As you perhaps infer, belongs to me;

There the 'Hospice des enfans-trouvés' stands;
Yet hundreds who have roamed through many lands
Have never seen, nor set a foot within it:
I'll whisk you thither in half a minute.

24.

" Behold that ancient, Convent-looking pile,
With garden laid out in becoming style;
The rooms are spacious, lofty, and well-aired,
No care is wanting, no expence is spared
To make the children happy; and they thrive,
Like bees within a comfortable hive.
If you could see their cradles in a row,
With cotton coverings, white as driven snow,
Your heart with kindly sympathy would glow;
That over-righteousness you oft display,
Like morning's mist would quickly melt away;
Your prudish virtues, which are sheer insanity,
You might exert, without the slightest vanity,
In such a cause as this—and serve humanity.

25.

" In Christian England, the returns have shown
That, only there, Infanticide is known;
Though ev'ry other crime abounds, and nurs'd is,
With that sad specialité it curs'd is.
Censure no longer, then, immoral France;
She is in some things wiser—in advance
Of all the world, as in the case of Foundlings,
Though it may shock the views of Saintly Groundlings
To know, ten thousand children, more or less,
Are annually rescued from distress,

Who, but for that good Priest, Vincent-de-Paul,
Had found no friend, had known no home at all;
Who, unprotected, growing up in vice,
To thieve or murder had not prov'd too nice.

26.

" Some day, John, seize a favorable chance;
Propose the plan that works so well in France:
No matter what the straight-laced, canting crew
May choose to think, or what they say of you.
Those acres in the Cromwell Road, just bought—
The very name of Noll inspires the thought—
Would be a splendid site for your design,
The soil is gravel, situation fine;
The Horticultural Gardens too are near,
Though those large cabbages they sell are dear;
Yet those fine Ladies who subscribe their guineas,
In which there surely neither harm nor sin is,
Might something give tow'rd those stray Piccaninnies.
There could be pasturage for cows, to milk,
Or asses, govern'd by Purveyor Dilke;
The boys might learn and practice naval gunnery,
The girls prepare for nursery or nunnery.
If you an opportunity let slip
To urge this point, I'll catch you on the hip.
There's room for canvass pictures, and for wood ones,
If they'll but burn the bad, and keep the good ones.
What are their Patents, Minerals, or Fossils,
Compared with girls and boys in caps and tassels?
I'm faint with all this arguing and talking,
We'll just descend; five minutes' easy walking
Will bring us to yon Abbey's ancient cloister,
Where we can get some chablis and an oyster."

27.

The sun has mounted in the glowing sky,
'Tis fever heat—a hot day in July;
The leaves look parch'd—no gently-stirring breeze
Is murm'ring softly through the neighbouring trees;
There is a stillness in the summer air
One scarcely hopes for at a Fancy Fair;
And no one at the Kensington Bazaar
Sees floating up on high that wond'rous car,
Though there are some long-sighted people present,
To whom a view of Lions would be pleasant.
So vast a group of Sœurs de Charité,
All bent on making some poor devil pay,
Ne'er met before, alms-seeking out of doors:
Grand Duchesses and Countesses by scores,
Hawking their trumpery wares with cunning skill,
Resolv'd to make you buy against your will.
In very art, these fashionable ones
Are more beseeching than the rudest Duns;
Far worse than Leeches, for, if once they stick,
They will phlebotomize you to the quick.
Men may escape a duel, or a battle,
Who cannot run from such engaging cattle,
To save five shillings for a baby's rattle.

28.

'Tis a sad state of things when blooming girls,
With full-blown cheeks and well-oiled amber curls,
Go Husband-hunting to these fairs and shows,
Some worthy object ever 'neath the rose.
There must be winning, charitable ways
In vending Drawings, Pincushions, Bouquets,

Which I am sure that Dandy Curate feels,
Who bends so low to beauty—all but kneels;
That well-cut coat of black, with upright collar,
Those gloves of lavender, which cost a dollar,
Those boots (they're French I swear) of patent leather,
Though nice, must hurt him in this sultry weather;
Yet, prattles he, and shows his teeth, pearl white,
As if his mortal frame thrill'd with delight;
His hat is glossy black, like bird in back-wood.
I wonder if the Parson writes in Blackwood!
That damsel in the spoon-like, nut-brown bonnet,
Would not object to read a well-penn'd sonnet
In praise of all her virtues and her charms,
Before she throw herself into his arms.
If wedlock be the game on which she ventures,
Let her beware before the church she enters;
Economy's the order of the day;
Fat livings will be scarce as Bishops die away.
Law, Physic, Army, Navy, *not* Devotion,
Will be the Key to plunder and promotion.

29.

Oh! lamentable sight! to grieve the heart,
Enamell'd, coloured, like some work of art,
Yon grinning Marchioness of sixty-three
A rosy maid of twenty tries to be.
Those teeth are false, without the pow'r to bite;
That wig hides hair of venerable white.
Deluded youth! whose purse must largely pay
For ices that those wither'd hands convey;
Each look that from those fishy eye-lids steals
The fever'd blood first stagnates, then congeals.

List to her voice! 'tis like some crack'd bassoon,
Or cry of owlet hooting to the moon;
Those flashing jewels which her neck inwreath
Mock but the shrivell'd parchment skin beneath;
Those feet in stocks, not boots, are ill at ease,
Unlike the Pilgrim's who had boil'd his peas.
Yet, such is Fashion—Folly! vain Endeavour!
The Rachel dogma, "Beautiful for ever."
To high-born sinners leave the dark disgrace
Of Nature outraging with painted face.
If such base gods the rich and proud adore,
Thrice bless'd are they, the simple and the poor!

30.

The fête is done—the crowd is growing thinner—
Folks *will* get hungry; then come thoughts of dinner.
Though our companions have grown quite relations,
They must look out somewhere for daily rations;
There are no difficulties in the way,
When voyageurs have got wherewith to pay;
'Tis but the place to fix on where to dine,
How many courses, and what sort of wine.
So Hudibras, with whom the choice or care is,
Decided they should go at once to Verrey's.

31.

"See! how they drive, those miserable elves!
As if the world belonged but to themselves;
Pell-mell go carriages of ev'ry kind,
Eager to leave their neighbours far behind:
God save the Crossers, be they deaf or blind!

We manage these things better down with us,
And if a soul's run over, make no fuss,
But hang the culprit without judge or jury,
Then throw his body to the nearest Fury.
I think in Russia 'tis, if an equestrian
Recklessly trample down a poor pedestrian,
They hand him to the Executioner's double,
And save the Coroner some time and trouble.
If such a law were put in force in London,
Few would escape—the butchers would be undone.
Jack Ketch would need to tuck them up in pairs;
He'd scarce find time to say his daily pray'rs."

32.

"Don't think," said Hudibras, as they sat dining,
"That I am giv'n to sadness, or repining;
There's not on earth, nor any where, a fellow
More kin to mirth, without being ever mellow.
Let me, pray, help you to my favorite dish,
A vol-au-vent of nice puff paste and fish.
This good white sauce, I feel disposed to say,
Would please the most fastidious Gourmet.
The French in cooking certainly excel.
Some wine, friend John! that is not bad Moselle.
Are you a Connoisseur in wines?"
"I'm not.
The grapes of Hungary and Greece have got
A flavour that I like. Professor Lie-big,
Whom some one designated once a sly pig,
Writes very strongly, praising up the former,
And adds, the wine is generous and warmer

Than many others."
"Yes! it is phosphoric:
My taste, I own, inclines to the caloric.
But you don't eat—here is a pudding—ice—
A contrast!"
"Just a taste! How very nice!
Though it does make my poor teeth tingle so!"
"A glass of Eau-de-vie or Curaçôa?"
"I fear to drink Liqueur, it is exciting."
"It may be; but 'tis ne'ertheless inviting:
One glass can do no harm."
"I'll try—here goes."
"Let's drink a toast. 'Straight jackets to our foes!'
Waiter! two cups of coffee, and the bill."
"The half is mine, remember."
"John! be still.
You are my guest, invited here to-day;
You'll have a chance some other time to pay."
"I've got some Green-backs!"
"Silence, for my sake."
"A five-pound Bank of England!"
"*That* they'll take!"
"John, I remember well the good old days
When notes bore Newland's name, and Henry Hase.
Old Abraham Newland was a better card
Than Abraham Lincoln."
"There you hit me hard!"
"Take money here! the bill is one pound three;
A half-a-crown for you. Now let us see—
It wants but half an hour to eight. All right!
Gounod's new Opera we'll go hear to-night.

"Opera!" responded John.
"Zounds! what's amiss,
That you stand so aghast?"
"'Tis simply this:
That I have scruples."
"Scruples! what d'ye mean?"
"I never was inside a Theatre seen."
"So much the better!"
"No! I cannot go."
"You shall, John—I insist."
"Well, be it so;
But I don't think it right, nor orthodox."
"Stuff! who's to see you? I've a private box,
Pit Tier."
"Of course that's down below?"
"Exactly!
It mounting saves, and one can sit compactly.
The entrance and the exit too are easy."
"Who sings to-night? I hope it will be Grisi!"
"No; Titiens sings, in Faust and Marguerite;
Giuglini too. You'll have a glorious treat!
So come along; you've got on a tail-coat:
I'm always *en costume* with this capote."

33.

In leaving Verrey's dining room, when full,
There's risk to give some lady's sleeve a pull,
Or be tript up by furbelows wide spread
Upon the carpet, as your way you thread.
It so befell. Things might have been much worse.
A *little* Dame, whose dress was the reverse,

Caught John's right foot, or rather *wrong* one—
It was a very large foot, and a long one—
And sent him sprawling on the floor. All laugh'd
But Hudibras, who knew they would be chaff'd.
" You must be Master of the Ceremony,
You so turn out your toes, and look so funny,"
Remark'd the female, as our fallen Knight
Before her bowed, in attitude polite.
" I crave your pardon; but your Crinoline
Is larger far than any I have seen.
Some inconvenience I perchance have caused;
The fault, no doubt, was mine."
The lady paused.
" Why! as I live—yes, it is Mister B.—
Who ever thought at Verrey's I should see
My dear, old, country friend?"
" John, come away!"
Said Hudibras, aside; " if here you stay,
I'll not be warrant for the consequences.
That's a young, cunning minx; right well she fences.
Her eyes are load-stars—come away!"
" You're right!"
But as he oped his lips to say good night,
The amorous damsel flung her arms around him,
And in her fond embrace so tightly bound him,
That it required some ready skill to part 'em;
Yet Hudibras did this " secundum artem."
With some disdain, she threw a glance on Nic:
" You have been guilty of a scurvy trick,"
Quoth she, " to thus so rudely interfere."
" I did not mean it rudely, Ma'am, I swear!"
" Well, since you say so," in familiar strain
She answered, " stand a bottle of Champagne!"

"Champagne!" cried John, good-humoured and
resign'd.
"Champagne!" replied his friend. "We have just
din'd!
And are engag'd to spend the evening out."
"I thought so! I know well what you're about:
You mean to take him to some gambling hell,
And win his money. Yes, I know you well.
Don't go!"
"I have agreed—but not to gamble."
"Ha! well—he'll lead you on a precious ramble.
He is a man would ne'er *my* fancy strike,
And has a sly expression I don't like."
Though this was said, in acting phrase, aside,
Nic heard it, and politely thus replied:
"Your blandishments much younger swains might
tempt;
But we from Love's sweet nonsense are exempt.
So, Madam, may your dreams be soft and light!
I and my Uncle wish you, modestly, good night!"

34.

But for that awkward, little contretemps,
Which so delayed them at the restaurant,
Our heroes would have heard the Ouverture.
Perhaps they did not lose much, to be sure.
At any rate, they were in time to hear
How Faust proposed to end his life's career
By drinking deep of that lethiferous spring
Which fails not to immortal slumber bring.
John the libretto took from out his pocket,
Just as the lamp was flickering in its socket.

But 'tis not in the power of beauty fair
To soothe a mind that's wedded to despair;
So falls the Maidens' Chorus to the ground,
While health and peace they to the youth propound.
Faust curses all, in manner most uncivil,
And summons to his aid the Prince of Evil.

35.

" Gracious!" exclaimed the wonder-stricken John,
As Mephistopheles glided slowly on;
" How like he is to you!"
" He has a firman
To travel always as my Cousin German.
Tho' that red cloak, black beard, and horn-peak'd cap,
Are too sensational—are but a trap
To catch the mob, to please the vulgar eye.
If *our* Costumier did such things, he'd die!
Defend me from such Managers as Harris,
Who trades in Lucifers and Fiends from Paris,
Importing ' Little Devils,' ' Satanellas,'
And blowing with a French-made pair of bellows
His fire and brimstone in a way provoking,
Authors and Actors, and the Audience, choking."

36.

Through five long, dreary, tiresome acts they waded,
And heard great Goethe's poem sore invaded.
John bore it all with positive good tact,
Till he beheld a sad and startling fact,
Occurring at the end of the third act;
Where Marguerite has whisper'd Faust good night,
And they have parted till the morning light.

Yet that young maiden, thinking it no sin,
Opens her chamber window, lets him in,
And at that moment, with her lover blest,
The curtain drops—and we may guess the rest.

37.

Twixt ev'ry act, great merriment they found,
In watching all the various groups around;
But naught aroused their mirth to such extent
As those gay dandies who the stalls frequent—
Those priggish coxcombs, over-dressed and frill'd,
Whose heads with ev'ry thing but brains are fill'd.
See! that old beau, almost too frail to stand,
Prying to know who's who, with glass in hand;
His wig and whiskers stick as close as brothers:
Truefit's the artist, who, above all others,
Excels in Succedaneums; he supplies
Hairs kin to those Dame Nature oft denies.
No one would dream that antiquated elf
Wore ebon locks he did not grow himself;
Though there are land-marks not to be gainsay'd,
That tell the voyages stern Time hath made,
Cosmetics and Columbian balm he thinks
Have closed up all the crevices and chinks.
Poor, driv'ling Dolt! there soon must come a crisis
To wean thee from thy follies and thy vices.
Be wiser! be contented with thy lot,
Nor strive to seem to be what thou art not.

38.

Hudibras rose—felt for his watch—'twas gone.
He smiled—'twas half a grin—exclaimed, "Why, John,

I have been robb'd! but not by you, I swear.
I now remember *when* it was, and *where:*
The fellow in the street who sold that book
My bréguet watch, and charms, most surely took;
Just as I turn'd me round, I felt a twitch,
And fancied that the scoundrel made a hitch;
No doubt but that his fingers were like pitch,
And any thing he chanc'd to touch would stick;
He knew his business—how to do the trick.
A London Pick-pocket is past belief;
Why *I'm* no match for your true Cockney Thief:
He'd take your eyes quite clean out for a lark,
And you'd not miss them were it in the dark.
But I've a Runner that, I think, can match him;
The Devil's *not* in it if I don't catch him."

39.

Our Opera friends had sounded a retreat
From box thirteen, o'ercome with thirst and heat.
The air outside was fresh—that breath of Heaven!
The hour not late, for some—half past eleven.
The Oxford Scholars, who've more gravity
Than Cantabs, know that, nearly vis-à-vis
With what we monogram as H. M. T.,
A Café stands. The Caffres hold a club there.
Why are they Unbelievers? None e'er snub there;
They only go, like other folks, to grub there.
There may be seen, not in the Caffre Chamber,
Gallants on town, and ladies dress'd in amber,
Enjoying devil'd chicken and champagne,
And cracking jokes *not* fresh-born in the brain.

Quoth Hudibras, " this is a novel sight;
That's why I bring you hither, John, to-night.
To yon snug-looking table follow me,
Where safe from all intrusion we shall be.
With just one bottle of the very best,
A lobster salad, in true manner drest,
We'll wind up our adventures of the day,
And criticize the music and the play."
Said John, " on one condition."
" Name it, pray."
" That I for supper be allowed to pay."
" Well, well, if you insist—are so partic'lar,
You shan't retort and say that I'm a stickler.
Here comes the supper; that's the style of thing!
I'll be the Minister, and you the King.

40.

" M. Gounod scores well, John, I must admit:
A Snip would call his garments a good fit.
But who cares half so much for clothes as form,
The living principle, inspired and warm,
The sweet, continuous strains that touch the heart,
Broad, flowing, like the music of Mozart?
Now Gounod's tunes (if tunes they be) are snatchy:
We'll coin another word to match it—patchy.
He wanders, too, about sometimes, as though
His mind were not made up where he should go.
Those ancient Burghers, with their beards in curl,
Who sang in praise of wine, or beer, or purl;
Those valiant Soldiers from the wars returning,
Whose breasts with love and glory still were burning,

Have got the Lion's share of Gounod's brain:
But I maintain it, and will say again,
There are few inspirations in his work.
The Waltz, I own, moves with a pleasant jerk;
The Soldiers' Chorus, "Gloria immortale,"
Is, in Italian rendering, "non c'è male."
Those rolling, large, Leviathan-like basses
Make up for weaker points in other places;
But Meyerbeer the Theme to Gounod hinted:
He's a rich mine for those whose means are stinted;
And "Su da bere" has, too, its twin brother;
And when you hear the one, you hear the other.
The Spinning-wheel Song is so slow and dull,
One knows not which to blame, the wheel or wool.
The ditty of King Thule, the flow'r and jewel,
Is most lugubrious, and long, and cruel,
A dish of very thin, weak water-gruel.
"Ei m'ama," which poor Marg'ret tries to warble,
When at her window, is as cold as marble.
No Bird-catcher can get a bird to stick,
Unless the Bird-lime be laid on quite thick.
If Faust had found in her no other charms,
That Song would ne'er have lured him to her arms.
Ergo, when Gounod gets a situation,
The truth comes out, he shows no inspiration.
"Saffo," "Saba," and others I forget,
Sisters in misery, whose sad eyes are wet
With weeping over non-success most sorely,
But illustrate his claim to Genius poorly.
It was too bad of that old Cynic, Chorley,
To thus mislead the Frenchman in his paper,
And laud and eulogize him so, and vapor,

Because a kind, good-tempered Publisher
Had—more's the pity!—ventured to incur
The risk of Faust in English, paraphrased
Like Gluck's Orféo, varnish'd, painted, glazed;
So that his nearest Kin, with perfect eyes,
The mutilated form can't recognize.

One need not, John, more words on this exhaust;
Monotony's the leading trait of Faust: [sures.
Three-four, six-eight, twelve-eight, his fav'rite mea-
Men may be crotchety e'en in their pleasures;
But that eternal marching in one pace
An air of dullness throws o'er time and space.
An ugly phrase or two, stuck here and there,
A contrast—that's it!—à la Meyerbeer,
Would much improve the music of the piece,
On which our strictures, for the present, cease.
As to the literary Incubation,
It is too worthless far for condemnation."

41.

"The supper's done, the bottle empty; so
With your permission we will pay and go.
While you arrange your cap and your capote, [note."
I'll get," quoth John, "some change for this Bank-
He scarce had left his boon companion's side,
Ere, with an eye of lightning, Nic espied
The same young Damsel of the dinner fray
Spring from a neighbouring box to watch her prey.

"Ha! ha! my friend's in danger! yet I'll cook her;
Yes, in the very nick of time will hook her."

With that he caught her, gave a graceful bend.
" I don't want you," she said ; " I want your friend."
And daggers look'd, as if she'd like to eat him.
" 'Tis well," he answered ; " I am going to meet him ;
So come along, my chambers are not far ;
A cup of Mocha and a prime Cigar
I've promised he shall have. But here he comes ! "
It was a sight to see John twist his thumbs,
As on the froward, pert, young dame he gazed,
Half pleased, half frightened, and yet much amazed.

" A word," quoth Hudibras to John, aside :
" This female friend of yours with me shall ride ;
To-morrow we shall meet. Do what I bid,
Or else of her you never will be rid.
I'll give my orders in a friendly way,
And you'll depart, pretending to obey.

As you prefer to walk to James's Square.
You'd better start ; I'll follow with the fair.
So toddle—quick ; if we have any luck,
We shall be there as soon as you, old Buck ! "

Tho' there seemed something to the girl mysterious,
She thought that all was strictly right and serious ;
Safe in a cab, the streets they rattled o'er,
And drove on till they reach'd a Bishop's door.
It being long past midnight, nearly one,
Nic told the Driver, in an under tone,
To gently knock ; meantime he handed out
The wondering Lady ; then turn'd right about.

Ere either could cry out Jack Robinson,
The gentleman in bottle-green was gone.

" He aint got through the key-hole," said the Cabby;
" But not to pay my fare was downright shabby."
" I won't go home," the Damsel cried, " that's clear,
Until I see his Uncle, who lives here."
With that she gave such a tremendous knock,
That the whole Square resounded with the shock.

A surly Porter, from his sleep disturb'd,
Who, living at a Prelate's, should be curb'd,
Look'd up the Area, and roar'd loudly out,
" Why, what the Devil's all this row about?"
" I want my friend!"
" What friend?" the Porter cried.
" The Uncle that I know," the Girl replied.
" Go to old Nick! we've got no Uncles here!
A Bishop is my master—he's a Peer!"

" A pretty Peer, to serve a woman so;
But till I see him, Sirrah! I'll not go!"
And as she clench'd her fist, the bell she rang,
And knock'd, resolv'd to still keep up the clang.
The Cabman, dreading something was amiss,
Responded, " I can't stand no more o' this;"
And like a prudent fellow drove away.
By this time there was seen a streak of day.
No Uncle ever came; she found no peace,
Till safe within the arms of the Police.

CANTO II.

1.

EASTWARD of Temple Bar we'll wing our way,
And change the venue, as the lawyers say.
The City man of forty years ago,
When manners were comparatively slow,
Beholds a difference in that trading mart,
In some respects so modern now and smart.
On week-days, all are busy as of yore;
Commerce still flogs the team, still plies the oar;
The active, restless, grasping money man
For gold still toils, makes all the wealth he can;
Capricious Fortune sometimes favor shows
To him who ventures, yet has nought to lose;
Shines on the plotting, reckless, gambling knave,
Whose ev'ry action is to Vice a slave;
While honest industry—the case is hard—
Meets, after years' of labour, no reward.

2.

Yes, those six, working days, out of the seven,
That as provision for man's wants are given,
Seem much the same in aspect now as then.
Long may the ancient City thrive! Amen!

Behold it on that solitary one day,
The Christian Sabbath designated Sunday!
Lonesome and tomb-like ev'ry street appears,
The place a strange, unwonted silence wears;
A human form is seldom ever seen,
As if some plague or pestilence had been;
Save at Saint Paul's, where country sinners come:
The other Saints might just as well be dumb—
So small the sect who care to hear them preach,
Or profit by the doctrines that they teach.
Churches abound—in ev'ry Lane are seen;
But Congregations "few and far between."
Yet do we hear a loud, continual cry,
A clamour for more churches, to supply
The spiritual wants of those, who care
Much more to breathe on Sundays purer air,
Than listen to a low-bred Scripture Reader,
Or counter-jumping Curate—a Seceder
From some Silk-warehouseman within the City.
If he should prove unletter'd, more's the pity!
" But this I know," quoth Hudibras, " the Church is
In danger, like unto a ship that lurches;
The waves of Skepticism are rolling round her:
If she have not good Pilots, she will founder.
She wants more eloquence, more Christian worth,
To wean frail, worldly-minded souls from earth.
Colenzo and the Catholics divide her;
Those seven Essays and Reviews deride her.
She must be up and stirring—lay aside
Her ancient rule of bigotry and pride,
Seek not to persecute the doubting mind
That labours only to conviction find.

If she believe her tenets to be true,
No need to use the torture or thumb-screw.
With pains and penalties she'll never make
A single Convert for Religion's sake.
Her prosecutions more than volumes speak,
Prove, spite her boasted strength, that she is weak;
Resembling that proud Pagan Race, who swore
Their fabled Gods a charm'd existence bore;
Yet thought it wise to clothe them still in armour,
Not to protect them, but to keep them warmer."

3.

" To Mother Church no mercy you have shown,"
Quoth John; " yet there is much that's true, I own.
The Sunday City dullness that prevails
Is owing to the Builders, and the Rails,
Those Lime and Plaster Locusts that alight
On ev'ry pretty, pleasant, verdant site,
And build what, in the advertising phrase,
Is called a Cottage orné in these days.

These Bricklayers are the greatest bane alive;
No wonder that but few of them e'er thrive.
No place is free, nor safe from their attacks;
From their rapacity they ne'er relax.
Trees that have taken centuries to rear,
Such as the untaught savages revere,
Trees that are bearing goodly, luscious fruit,
These ruthless monsters tear up, branch and root.
For miles round London there will not be seen
A fertile valley, nor an acre green,

If some enactment be not shortly made
To curb these fellows in their wanton trade.
Just look at Kensington, by the Queen's gate,
And note those mansions that for tenants wait,
But fit for you, or some great Minister of State."

" Let them alone, John; they will lose their pelf;
Your over-building always cures itself.
We've had such doings in the lower sphere;
But 'twas not worth my while to interfere.
These chaps will find their level some fine day,
In houses they won't build themselves—of clay."

4.

John straight continued: " I was just now saying
That, while their City mansions were decaying,
Or empty, wanting air and ventilation,
Your London Merchant, near some railway station,
Has got his country box, his seat, or villa,
With some grand name, Romilius or Quintilla;
Seneca Lodge and Cato's Cot I've seen
Somewhere in Addison Road, or Parson's Green.
'Tis quite as natural as for silly folks
To name their houses, Lindens, Cedars, Oaks,
When there is not a tree. That *is* a hoax
On poor, misguided strangers and their betters—
Much worse, if they engrave it on their letters!"

" 'Tis clear," said Hudibras, "twixt Rails and Builders,
There's been some work for what the Dutch call *guilders*.
I like not either: I think both a curse;
For one defaces Nature, and, what's worse,

Sends thousands unanointed to Jones Davy,
Ere they have time to say a single Ave.
Their lines *above* the earth are full—no wonder
They are delving, digging, diving under.
I neither warn, nor offer an opinion;
But if they trench one inch on my dominion,
I'll send them flying soon, in different ways,
And illustrate the system of Trappèze.

5.

" Visit the Crystal Palace in July!
We'll go, John; it is open, wet or dry.
The screen that they call Tropical 's pull'd down.
Is that some flash term, only used in town?
Perhaps it means that, now there is *no* screen,
We can see *something*—something's to be seen.
I read, ' the Gardens radiant are with flow'rs.'
Why! in description they must rival ours.
' The Ro-se-ry,' or ' Ro-sa-ry'—which way
Would Lindley Murray write or spell it, pray?—
' With bloom is covered, and the fine collection
Of plants and trees is now in full perfection.'
Of course the Manager invites inspection.
Then there are fountains forced from water-pails."
" I've seen," quoth John, " the fountains at Versailles,
Which gush, and upward mount unto the skies.
It *is* a sight to see *those* fountains rise—
A sight enough to glad a Frenchman's eyes."
" You must not under-rate the English, John;
In Hydrostatics they rank number one:
In Hydropathics, with a little gin slow;
In Hydrophobia, with Professor Winslow.

To ev'ry sort of Hydra with a name
They may, with right and justice, lay a claim.

"But here we are, just at our journey's end,"
Cried Hudibras.
"Not yet, my ancient friend!
We've got no end of steps still to ascend."
"Steps are my horror! my supreme disgust!"
Quoth Hudibras. "Your modern Builder must
Ape those who reared the Pyramids and Babel.
How, in the course of nature, is one able,
If e'en to getting up the stairs inclined,
Or were, as Dr. Johnson says, in wind,
To climb, when one has fully lunch'd or dined?"

"You ne'er have been in Edinboro town,
Or you would see the law of up and down
Most beautifully followed in a Flat
Some thirteen stories high—mark that!"
Said John.
"A Flat in Scotland! I ne'er heard,"
Quoth Nic, "of aught so monstrous or absurd.
The Scotch proverbially are so sharp,
That e'en a man who only played the Harp—
The Jew's-harp was the instrument he play'd—
Swore that he could not to a profit trade,
They were so canny and so clever.
Yes, that poor Jew, who cried '*ajew!* for ever.'
In after times, whene'er he touch'd his harp,
Would sigh and say, 'them Scotch they are so sharp!'"
"You have confounded flats with floors," said John;
"But we are up—so say no more thereon."

" I swear, by Baden Baden and Brook Green,
This is a spot most lovely to be seen!
Had Robins lived to view a place like this,
He would have called it ' the Abode of Bliss.'
I do not commentate," quoth Nic, " like Blackstone;
But, judging fairly between Fowke and Paxton,
The one is light, fantastic, as some fairy;
The other neither light, nor tight, nor airy.
The view from this Balcony where we stand
Is fine, extensive; some would call it grand.
Far as the eye can scan the landscape bright,
Some pleasing object meets the wandering sight,
Valley or streamlet, wood or distant height.
Here might the Lover in his Mistress' ear
Pour the soft music she delights to hear.
Here might the Poet idly, fondly stray,
And wake his lute to love or glory's lay:
Here may the young, with buoyant spirits fill'd,
Their fancied visions, airy castles build:
Here may the old, forgetting care and pain,
The scene enjoy, breathe life's glad air again:
Here may the toiling Artisan retreat
From busy labor—find a refuge sweet.
Yes; to behold a peaceful spot like this,
'Tis something surely kin to human bliss."

6.

Hudibras would have prosed till close of day,
Had John not gently wiled his steps away.
Within the Palace, wondering with amaze,
Above, beyond, on ev'ry side they gaze:

Fountains and Flow'rs, and countless Statues, seem
To realize some glowing, fabled dream.
As they the gay Alhambra Court explore,
And view its richly tesselated floor,
The Travellers, with a mutual instinct, threw
A parting look, and silently withdrew.

7.

" Friend John, the paintings in this Picture Gallery
Afford, methinks, some scope for fun and raillery.
I've seen far better things than any of them—
At least, to qualify, than many of them—
Gracing a modest, country, road-side Inn,
Where they sell sloes for Port, vitriol for Gin.
That green stuff is not grass; those bulls arn't beeves;
Those Saints are not like old Salvator's thieves;
That kirtled maiden, feigning to seem shy,
Has got a laughing devil in her eye.
Just look upon that water, and that mill!
'Tis not surprising that large wheel stands still:
The paint upon the stream is laid so thick,
It can't go round; ergo, the thing must stick.
Bless me! a field of battle that pourtrays;
Horses and men are placed in awkward ways.
Who a left-handed swordsman e'er did see?
That hero's head is where his feet should be.
One of those gambling boors in that Dutch group
Is playing with his cards turn'd wrong way up.
That head of Holofernes is the work
Of some Sign-painter, neither Jew nor Turk.
If Mistress Potiphar had no more charms,
To lure her House Comptroller to her arms,

Than those the artist here has painted in,
'Tis not a marvel Joseph did *not* sin.
If there be any pictures more sublime
Than these, John, we must come another time.

8.

" That's the great Organ, is it ? "
" Yes," quoth John ;
" Founded by Messieurs Gray and Davison.
Coward they say's a rara avis on
The instrument ; few organists play better ;
He knows the use of pedals to the letter,
And ev'ry stop, and *when* to stop, to please.
Besides, he is so perfectly at ease,
So much at home on all those rows of keys,
Has ev'ry subject ready at a call,
From wedding march to that dead one in Saul ;
He loves the classical, and knows by heart
Bach, Handel, Haydn, Mendelssohn, Mozart.
Yet will he sometimes kindly condescend
To please the audience and oblige a friend ;
And sport, like some wing'd spirit of the air,
With Herold, Verdi, Meyerbeer, Auber ;
Or like a new fish, Delphin, or Delphini,
Wanton and play with soul-inspired Rossini.
Listen ! he's just beginning."
" We'll sit down,"
Said Hudibras, " by this young Quaker Girl in brown."

The theme he chose would not have pleas'd a waiter,
Nor those who for the Canterbury cater :
Not speaking broadly, 'twas the " Stabat Mater."

When "Il gran Maestro" "Pro peccatis" penn'd,
He little dreamed his sacred work would end
In some old Scribbler, who is living still,
Turning the air into a vile quadrille.
I've heard, a wag once strongly recommended
The scape-grace Sinner, who had so offended,
To throw into the pot a few more faults,
And add the Elijah Polka and Messiah Waltz.

9.

In ev'ry place whereon the sun doth shine,
The thirsty still will drink, the hungry dine.
In that long room that overlooks the garden,
Where dines a youthful Ward with her old Warden,
Off usual fare, cold chicken, or veal pasty,
Our Comrades lunch'd, in fashion somewhat hasty
For good digestion—though each appetite
Was sharp: it seemed as if they ate in spite.

The wine was but so so—the cheese quite sour;
The bread was dry—the alum dried the flour.
The Waiter too was drunk, and most uncivil;
But then he did not know he waited on the Devil:
And paying but five shillings for a meal
That's not worth half a crown is a good deal.
What must the profit be, twixt host and tartar,
At the Freemasons, and the Star and Garter
On Richmond Hill, where once there liv'd a lass,
Who did, the Song says, ev'ry maid surpass?
I have a sort of tremor at dear dinners:
Poor Richard thought the guinea-a-head-folks sinners

10.

" More music, John ?"

" The Crystal Palace Band.
Not in the *great* Orchestra—that's *too* grand
For Manns and his slow, sleepy Minuets;
The managers reserve that for their pets,
M. Costa and the Handel Choir, who sing
On State Occasions, once a year; yet bring,
Alas ! no grist unto the mill, I fear;
Although the entrance is made very dear.
They might find less expensive pets, I think,
That would not cause the Palace funds to shrink.
But *very* great folks are not eas'ly guided,
Especially if they should be *one*-sided.
They have a treat, too, for their friends in low church,
Something beneath the City belles of Bow church.
Two thousand little girls, as many boys,
Not clothed in Angels' frames, but corderoys,
The scent of which would baffle Rimmel's nose
To say if it were Jessamine or Rose.
Their durability I do not doubt;
But, ah ! their fragrance is past finding out.
Shut all the doors against these children's coming,
Lay by their psalmody and sacred humming,
Stop those pianos' everlasting strumming;
Banish all Acrobats and Necromancers,
Blondins and Leotards, and tight-rope dancers.
Reduce, not raise, the prices, just to please
The Seasoners who live at home at ease,
Who only come on Saturdays to squeeze,
To show their dresses, flounc'd and cut, and starr'd,
And strut like peacocks in a poultry yard.

Build a new room for music somewhere near,
Where all the Concert-loving folks can hear.
We want no galleries, nor Directors' lodges,
Nor any other artificial dodges.
Your thorough Artist thinks it *not* a treat
To pay a half-crown extra for a seat,
Howe'er reserv'd; there should be no such thing, in
Places expressly made to play and sing in.
Your easy chair and padded leathern stall
Are but unmanly luxuries, after all,
Fit but for fuddled Critics, or old Women,
Or any other Ogre to look grim in.
The more that from such weaknesses we keep,
Less chance there'll be for audiences to sleep.
I've watch'd a dame, who prais'd Beethoven's score,
At Hallé's, fast asleep—have heard her snore!
If Churches once indulge in easy chairs,
The flock will rather nap than say its pray'rs.
Effeminacies of all sorts will grow,
When once the seeds of indolence we sow.
Your clubs, your limited joint-stock hotels,
Are but resorts where sensual pleasure dwells:
Not pleased to dine at home, the modern glutton
Would scorn to feed on vulgar beef and mutton;
He dotes on entrées, sweet-breads, and ragoûts,
Smacks his coarse lips while doubting which to choose.
So day by day the feasting vice goes on,
Till the too stimulated appetite is gone.
The Roman Apicii were not a fable,
Excelling in excesses of the table;
Tiberiuses, Vitelliuses, are living,
Walking the streets of London, fat and thriving;

Of Heliogabaluses a number,
Whose gormandizing faculties ne'er slumber,
Whose worthless lives are spent in eating, drinking,
Their brute desires unfitting them for thinking."

" Ha! John, your early, sacred-history Sinners,
Who worshipped Idols as some worship dinners,
Were far behind the culprits of our day;
They might be reckoned Angels in their way;
For whate'er failings they possess'd, beside
Lust, hardness, stubborness of heart, and pride,
They were not so insatiable in crime
As some who figure in our own good time.
They really had a small vocabulary,
As could be proved by our Constabulary.
If fire and brimstone swept away that nation,
I quake, John, for the present generation.
What's posted yonder?"

John replied, " a Bill!
" I'll step and read it, if you'll but sit still."
" Some new temptation for poor souls!" Nic cried.
" These English are with ev'ry thing supplied.
Well, John, what is it?"

" It's a Fancy Fair!"
" Another Fancy Fair! Good gracious! Where?"
" Held here—an annual thing—a tax on knowledge,
A grand bazaar for the Dramatic College."
" Dramatic what?"

" A College for poor actors."
" What! have they found at last, then, Benefactors?
The Actor whom the Law terms ' Vagabundus,'
Who tragedy, and comedy, and fun does,

May find, when strength shall fail and sight grow dim,
When age is paralysing ev'ry limb,
A shelter for his bones, a haven blest,
Wherein the stricken wanderer may rest?
He who pourtraying with a magic art
The tenderest passions of the human heart,
He who hath waked some soul to sympathy,
And brought the trembling tear to beauty's eye,
Or with a merry humour, bright as day,
Chased some corroding sorrow far away;
On some desponding face lit up a smile
That made the sad one happy for a while?
Oh! it were hard, if he whose life hath been
One course of labor on this mimic scene,
Whose best exertions through the live-long night
Were given to cheer us, to instruct, delight,—
'Twere hard, if he, in his declining day,
In want and wretchedness should pass away."

12.

" There's one thing," John replied, " that shocks, appalls:
The Actresses are all ranged round in Stalls,
Smiling and smirking, very smart and nice;
They sell not at 'alarming sacrifice';
The things they vend fetch an alarming price.
What think you? Lydia Thompson only blows
A kiss upon a common, cabbage rose,
And asks five shillings for it!"
" You believe it?"
" I do—I know that there are fools who'd give it."

" I'd like to see you, John, in such a trap,
Bargaining for some small baby frock, or cap;
Or garters highly scented with the Otto
Of Roses, with a ' Pensez à moi ' motto.
If then the Actresses get so much money,
What do the Actors?"
" They are very funny.
Paul Bedford plays, in one of Chorley's pieces,
' The tongueless Bell-man and his injured Nieces.'
After a combat, on the village green,
With the unknown Seducer, who's unseen,
The Bell-man dances on a rope of sand,
Without a pole, a Spanish Saraband;
When, suddenly, the bells ring from the steeple,
Amidst the vivas of the wondering people,
A man is seen to drop from the church spire,
His large and flowing mantle all on fire;
He just has time to scorch the Bell-man's nieces,
Who die—the Bell-man tumbles into pieces."

13.

" Buckstone, the Author-Actor, and some others,
Assist like Corsican dramatic brothers,
And coax adventurous heroes to their alley,
To have a throw with sticks at poor Aunt Sally.
Shillings and strokes in numbers they must wipe out,
Ere they succeed to put Aunt Sally's pipe out.
More methods still they try, the funds to raise;
Their vast inventions are beyond all praise."

' But I hear nought," quoth Nic, " of Shakspeare's
No scene, no reading, worthy of his fame. [name,

Dramatic Art, without its Master God,
Is but mock worship to a lifeless clod.
Endowments, Colleges, are noble things,
A lustre add to Governments and Kings;
But he whose genius vivified the mass,
The mighty Wizard, whose enchanted glass
Revealed the hidden treasures of the mind,
Shall he no niche among their revels find?"

14.

"His matchless works," adroitly added John,
"Are monuments enough to look upon—
Colossal, grand, instructive, vast,
That scarcely seem in human models cast.
Though we have other bards and minstrels reared,
Shakspeare's the noblest still, the most revered;
His writings, like the sacred book sublime,
Have stood the test of Text-books and of Time:
From Pole to Pole his varied labors fly,
Teeming with truths immortal that can never die."

15.

"And yet," quoth Hudibras, "is't not disgrace
That one unrivalled, holding such a place
In men's affections, should, alas! be spurned?
Like some dull volume quietly inurned?
His tragedies, and comedies, and plays,
Find readers few in these degenerate days.
A monster-loving, weak, unnatural age
Has banished Shakspeare from the English stage,
And substituted trash, mere Fungi, spawn,
As 'Peep of Day,' 'Duke's Motto,' 'Colleen Bawn.'

From such unwholesome food 'tis hard to choose
Twixt *Fricandeaux* and coarse Hibernian Stews."

16.

" There's some anomaly in this," John cried;
" Because I read—perhaps the papers lied—
That Hamlet, with new scenery and dresses,
Was very lately played at the Princess's.
The hero of the piece was a none-such,
A German, Frenchman, or low Dutch;
I know not which, from lack of thought or wit,
But heard he made a most tremendous hit,
And that Miss Burdett Coutts, or Coutts Burdett,
The foreign Actor's sails had flowing set;
That Kemble, and the Keans, both old and young one,
Were sticks compared with this new-sprung one.
The Critic, though it might be special pleading,
Cited some novel points, too, in the reading."

17.

" John! if you trust to Criticisms in papers,
Those vapid fancies, unsubstantial vapors,
Those Jack o' Lanterns that appear at night,
Or, rather, with the early morning's light,
The produce of some gaseous, not *sa*-gacious brain,
You will be duped, and little knowledge gain.
Why, I once knew a Critic, so they called him—
Gods! since that time how they have mauled him!—
Well dress'd, to outward eyes a swell quite,
Though in his heart a ravenous, hungry Hell-kite,
Without the talent e'en to read or spell right;

Yes, I have known that scurvy fellow send
A notice, systematically penn'd,
Of a performance of the Traviata,
Wherein the Donna, his Inamorata,
Was lauded to the skies. But, mark the sequel!
His judgment and his juggling were not equal:
The Traviata whom he raved about
Did not, for reasons known, that night come out.
The owners of the paper, caught thus tripping,
Paid the poor Devil his fee, and sent him skipping—
And serv'd him right."
"I think so too," quoth John.
"I've more to add," said Hudibras.
"Go on!"

18.

"The Geniuses—excuse me if I smile,
The term is common in Britannia's Isle—
Who scribble of the Concert Room and Stage,
May nothing know of Art; they but engage
To furnish matter at so much per line:
A penny *was* the price in days lang syne.
Perhaps high rents, and higher style of living,
Have raised the terms; though I have some misgiving
Whether the stuff, in quality or size,
Be worth so much if sold for truth, as lies.
Your modern Novelist, who travels further,
Revels in Incest, Bigamy, and Murder;
A large amount of crime his work discloses;
He tries minute, infinitesimal doses,
Like Homeopathic doctors, or old Nero;
No matter how, he always kills his hero,

And, like a clever, thorough man of parts,
Deals very much with black-guards and black arts.

19.

"John, you're accounted shrewd, have much discretion;
If *I* have got a fault, it is digression :
But this I know, I'm coming to the point,
The times are growing sadly out of joint,
When foreigners are hired to Shakspeare act,
To hear each sentence mouth'd and maul'd, and hack'd
To pieces. London Managers are crack'd !
And what are English Audiences, who sit
In private boxes, gallery, stalls and pit,
Aiding, abetting, murder loudly lauding,
'Murder most foul, as in the best it is,' applauding?
'Sdeath ! they can hear their mother tongue so spoken,
Shamefully, wrongfully, mutilated, broken,
Torn into fragments, open'd into chasms,
Doled out as if the Actor were in spasms?
Vowels and simple sounds, if right in pitch,
One knows not 'who is who, nor which is which' ;
The A's are O's, the marble Slabs are Slobs,
And Blanche is sounded Blonche, and Blabs are Blobs.
The Stage deserves dis-odour and disgrace,
When Shakspeare to Sensation filth gives place.

20.

"The time may never come to you, nor me,
A rightful state of things in Art to see.
Till we have Legislators who'll advance
Dramatic matters as they do in France,

And found a School for Music, Elocution,
With ample means, *not* private contribution;
Till then, our actors never will be better,
Our vocalists ne'er learn to know a letter.
Excepting very few among all classes,
I think your Singers are consummate asses;
For, if their lungs but happen to be strong,
And they can bellow into ears as long,
Applause must follow, as night follows day,
And Fortune smile with her all-cheering ray.
They're soon beyond all human aid or reach,
Too proud to profit from those skill'd to teach;
They shout and bawl, and bawl and shout the more,
While vulgar Country Clowns cry out encore:
Method, expression, style, is nothing worth,
Your *singing* fool 's the greatest fool on earth.

21.

" John, the American mail has just come in,
With news from Washington and Abraham Lin:
They still hold forth the Southerns cannot win.
One scarce knows which of them to most deride,
The President, or those who, on his side,
Are fighting against brother, against friend,
In a bad cause, too bad, alas! to mend.
To free the Slave, at least from Southern yoke,
They cry—believe it is a master-stroke
Of policy—while they would use the thong,
Would bind him still in fetters far more strong;
Or, if they made him free, 'twould be to arm
Him, spread more mischief, cause more dread alarm,

Goad the misguided Serf to shed the blood
Of those who his best, truest friends had stood.
Shame! on the recreant knaves, who, as a plea,
Adopt the canting phrase, Humanity.

Compare the Southern Slave with those who breathe
The poisonous atmosphere of mines beneath,
Who toil and sweat, with slight or no repose,
Till life is burdensome, or weary grows.
Look in the mills that keep your Cotton Lords,
See there the old, the young, the countless hordes
Of squalid, half-starved, miserable elves,
Almost afraid to look upon themselves;
With tattered, greasy garments on their backs,
With minds as barren as the desert tracks,
They scarce look human, yet the Preacher prates
In praise of them, compared to those on Slave estates.

22.

" Stump Orators, like Beecher Ward, may bawl
Their shallow notions in some Temperance Hall,
And pack each hole and corner of the place
With unwash'd louts of doubtful creed or race,
Then trumpet to the world 'A glorious greeting!'
'A grand ovation!' 'A triumphant meeting!'
Uniting the stale cry. 'The Peace Pretence!'
Where is the Wealth, the Rank, Intelligence
Of England, while these mummers rave
About Emancipation to the Slave?
Laughing that ever men could be such fools
As listen to the teachers of such schools.

Who sent that Yankee Fanatic, old Ward,
To preach? He should be *striped* as well as starred.
His blust'rings and his blasphemies are vile,
Though they attention rivet for the while.
The wicked Ruler of the Agapemone
Ne'er likened to the Garden of Gethsemane
The Trials of the North, as he has done;
Nor offered up, as Abram did his Son,
His boys a ready sacrifice to War.
This sort of preaching 's going rather far.
If in his ardent nature he inherit
A tithe of young King David's warlike spirit,
Let him be ransom for each hapless wight,
Release his boys, and go himself to fight:
He might in Fame's bright lap get really *sunn'd*,
Nor rank upon the 'Secret Service Fund.'
A fit Expounder of the Holy Word
Is he who advocates the fire and sword!
Who feeds the flame his Sister Stowe first raised,
When 'Uncle Tom' and Northern worth she praised;
Whose doctrines, spite of all his outward zeal,
A most unchristian principle reveal.
Go back to thy own Land, the Land of Strife,
Thy Heralds be the Torch and Bowie-knife."

23.

"'Tis not your Yankee in his patent boots
Who cares to fight," said John, "but savage brutes
From Ireland, Holland—Mercenaries base,
Who any land or country would disgrace;
Without a spark of honor in their breasts,
Fighting for love of blood, like to wild beasts;
The hangman's rope should be such miscreants' crests.

Once I had hopes that Palmerston and Russell
Would put an end to this unholy tussle.
But Poland, and New Zealand, and Japan,
Are quite enough to scare the boldest man.
Wars are like Law-suits, ever doubtful cases;
The Plaintiff and Defendant oft change places:
They yield no solid wealth to their employers,
And benefit but Powder Mills and Lawyers."

24.

"Oh! I have watch'd," said Hudibras, "this struggle,
Seen how those Northerners have tried to juggle,
To lie and shuffle, and with vain conceit
Striv'n to conceal their merited defeat.
While their opponents, chivalrous and brave,
Have baffled, routed them on land and wave;
Though scant in number, poorly clothed and fed,
Their dauntless ranks, by valiant chieftains led,
Have triumph'd o'er the fierce, Barbarian Host,
Whose vaunted prowess is, at best, a boast.
Yes! hearts that fight as southern hearts have fought,
For home and freedom, danger set at nought.
If victory were, by chance, to crown their foes,
It would not bring the contest to a close,
While there remained one Southern arm to wield
A weapon, or one man to take the field.

25.

"Ere long, the Demon Discord will arise
In their proud, northern city. Lurid skies
And ringing rifles soon will there proclaim
Riot and Rapine have begun their game.

The helpless Negro, hated then the more,
Refuge will strife to seek from door to door;
Hunted like some poor hare, in vain he'll fly,
The lawless mob will doom the wretch to die.
'Free the poor Slave!' 'Break Slavery's Chain!'
Cry Abolitionists in maw-worm strain,
While Lincoln cracks his jokes and drinks Champagne.

26.

"But they have hatch'd an evil that will grow
With giant strength, and speedily o'erthrow
Their sanguine hopes; the vast Conscription laws
Will fail; Men will not fight in such a cause:
Recruits, obtained but at the cannon's mouth,
Will rather aid, than war against the South.

Where are the ninety Seward Days? Vain boast!
Where the great Generals? Where their federal host?
Widows and orphans vainly wail and weep,
While husbands, fathers, lie in death's cold sleep.
Fastings and prayers are offered up the while,
For so-called victories, at the funeral pile.

With blind, besotted policy, they dream,
And harbour still a wild Utopian scheme,
That once again the Union flag will wave
O'er their doom'd city. May it prove the grave
Of ev'ry whining hypocrite and knave,
Whose love of lucre prompted first the cry
Against the unoffendiug Slave and Slavery!"

27.

" If I were Lincoln," John said, " at this crisis,
I'd free myself from all these mean devices :
Emancipation, confiscation acts, and worse
Than all, the foul conscription—'tis a curse!
And must fall heavy on the head and brisket
Of him who has the hardihood to risk it.
Why, with all his discomfitures, disasters,
Will he resort to these quack doctors' plaisters?
Try ev'ry Dulcamara's specious nostrum?
Give ear to ev'ry fool that mounts the rostrum?
Better resign; or, better still, make peace,
And let this hated, murderous warfare cease.
He might retire and earn a Conqueror's laurels,
Or join the Mormons and improve his morals.
Brigham would hail him in the Salt Lake City,
And help him to a wife or two, if fit he
Could prove himself to govern *more* than one:
The chances are, he would let well alone.
The man who rashly multiplies his wives,
In virtuous England, very rarely thrives;
One wife's a dose in that capricious clime,
Enough for any constitution at one time.
Yet Brigham Young is reckoned wise and thrifty,
And, by the last accounts, he had got fifty.

28.

" John, of such subjects we've had quantum suf.
Have you your box? I think a pinch of snuff
Would ease my nerves; I feel they're somewhat shaken,
That Yankee fire has wellnigh cooked my bacon."

"I have no box, and snuff is filthy stuff."
"Indeed! I always thought you up to snuff."
"No; I can smoke a clay pipe or cigar;
But taking snuff is rather below par."
"Men's noses are not chimneys it is true,"
Quoth Hudi, "though one smoke till all be blue."
With that, he drew out, first, his red bandanna,
Then handed John a prime, old, genuine Havanna.

29.

Very fine folks, with very fine white chokers,
May turn their noses up at two true smokers;
Pretending great disgust for both to feel,
Adding, perhaps, "'tis very ungenteel
To smoke where Ladies are, or where they may be."
Such individuals are the Genus—Gaby!
The greatest men of whom we ever read
Were famous smokers, loved the fragrant weed:
Newton, Locke, Bacon, Pope, Parr, Swift, and Hobbes,
Puff'd and philosophized, like thorough Nobs;
Their careless fingers gracefully were placed
Around the long pipe's snowy waist:
Soothed and subdued, the tranquil, happy mind
To pleasant labor felt itself inclined;
The depths of science calmly were explored;
The Muse, inventive, on proud pinions soared;
The merry wag, 'mid wreaths of curling smoke,
Conceived a pun, brought forth a witty joke.
The first Napoleon, War's great Engine Stoker,
Was an inveterate snuffer and a smoker.
His soldiers copied him in the Bivouack,
And sang the praises of "*la pipe tabac.*"

We have had Kings, such as King James the First,
Who wrote against it, and the practice curs'd.
He wasn't, perhaps, the wisest, nor the worst
Of monarchs, and so we may e'en forgive him;
No matter *what* he wrote, we don't believe him.
Elizabeth, and Ladies of her nation,
Indulged in smoking, which was then the fashion;
And Raleigh, who at pipes was an old stager,
Once made a bet—nay, more, he *won* the wager.
The Queen had ventured him a purse of gold
Against his Barbary Courser, so 'tis told,
That he should weigh his bacco, and not say
The true amount of smoke that pass'd away.

30

" I've smoked it," Raleigh cried; " the pipe is done."
" Then weigh the smoke," the Queen said, full of fun.
" I will," the Knight replied. The scales he took
From off a neighbouring table in some nook.
" Behold, your Majesty, with little pains,
The weight of ashes that the pipe retains.
If from the unburnt herb you it subtract,
You'll find the produce of the smoke exact."

" The purse is thine, the laugh belongs to thee,
For, truly, thou art more than match for me.
Many there be who fiery aid invoke,
Whose endless labors ever end in smoke;
But thou art one as clever as thou'rt bold,
The first whose smoke was ever turn'd to gold."

31.

" We have great Weedsters in our own good day,"
Quoth John; " distinguished Authors in their way,
Hardworking men, whose labors never cease,
Who joy to smoke the Calumet of peace.
Two at this very moment I have hit on,
Vanity Thackeray and Sir Bulwer Lytton.

One of our Royal Dukes, who was a Sage too,
Had pipes of ev'ry clime and size, and age too;
He had an Eastern, twenty yards in length,
Conducted through a wall of decent strength;
Turkish, of red clay, with tube of cherry-stick,
Some very short ones, that made you very sick;
German and French ones, call'd " écume de mer";
Dutch and American—the last would make you stare;
Once it a murderous Tomahawk had been,
Though on its bowl no gouts of blood were seen.

32.

" Pray what became of them?" cried Nic, with wonder;
" They would have proved a splendid source of plunder.
One should respect the phrase ' tuum et meum';
But, still, I very much would like to see 'em."

33.

John gave a sigh—" alas! they've had their day!
The pipes are out, the Duke is turn'd to Clay!"

CANTO III.

1.

East, west, north, south, whcre'er your footsteps roam,
There, there they are, secure to find a home;
In streets, in lanes, the Burlington Arcade,
In shops, bazaars, where'er you chance to trade;
On Sundays, week-days, morning, noon, and night,
The same eternal family greets the sight;
If through the Parks you stray to take the air,
One of the like fraternity is there;
Driving thro' Hampton, Richmond, Turnham Green,
Riding where seldom travellers are seen,
In cities, towns, in villages or hamlets,
Clothed in all guises, Blouses, Cloaks, and Camlets,
Look up, look down, on right hand, or on left,
Ascend a mountain, or peep through a cleft,
Shooting or fishing, strolling by the sea,
Picnicing, pleasuring, as the case may be,
Rail-road or river, traverse earth or air,
Still you behold them ever, ever there:
Swarming like locusts, countless as the stars,
Fair ones and dark ones, Lovers and Lascars,

Long, lean, and lanky, angular and round,
Fat, fresh, and frouzy, blooming and unsound,
Colours of the rainbow, black, white, and grey,
Spring-time and Autumn, January, May,
Pride, Lust, and Avarice, Vice of ev'ry shade,
Wit, Virtue, Wisdom, side by side displayed,
All that is noble, ev'ry thing that's base,
Youth, Age, and Beauty, ev'ry form and face,
Mothers and fathers, children, giants, dwarfs,
Turbans and tunics, mantles, shawls, and scarfs:
East, west, north, south, on mountain, or on wave,
Like ghosts they come to haunt us from the grave,
Cold, dull, and speechless, corse-like still they look,
Whether on wall, in window, or in book;
There is no balm, no reverential food,
That one can take to do the body good;
However shunn'd, however much despised,
The foul malignants won't be exorcised;
They point, they telegraph in various ways,
Some withered finger ever meets the gaze;
Go where you will, it is of no avail;
Like Indian hunters, they are on the trail:
The Cannibal, that eats man, woman, child,
The thorough Savage in untrodden wild,
The Hermit in his deep and lonely cell,
The Gnomes that in earth's inner regions dwell,
May have escaped those monsters ranged on pegs,
That horrid progeny of arms and legs,
Hatch'd by the sun, like Cocatrice's eggs;
But we, alas! must meet the hideous stare
Of those mis-shapen eyes that falsely glare,

Be doomed the hard, strong, granite lines to trace
Of each expressionless, unmeaning face;
While the Arch Fiend, who at our misery laughs,
Cries, "there they are! there! there! those Photographs!"

2.

Before the closing of the Opera houses,
Ere grouse-destroying husbands quit their spouses,
If, about four, you chance to walk or drive
Down Regent Street, the place is like a hive;
You feel convinced that London is alive.

'Twas then our two companions stroll'd, *not* walk'd;
Much might they think, but very little talk'd.
Halting at Mayall's, where the portraits, framed,
Hang out so nicely, are so wisely named,
To save all doubt if it's a Sphinx or Lion,
An aged father Oak, or sprouting Cion,
You see there quite a bevy of great people,
Some who comptrol the Stage, and some the Steeple;
Buckstone, as large as life, distempered o'er;
Bishops, with wet-nurse aprons pinn'd before;
Gladstone, as if he had been taxed to sit;
Sir Wentworth Dilke, with stomacher to fit;
Others with queer, hard names, and harder features,
Who, in Statistics, number as God's creatures,
Who "go for men" among life's human Cogs,
As "demi-wolves are cleped all by the name of Dogs."

3.

" Why, John," quoth Hudibras, " who would have
guess'd
To find your portrait figuring with the rest?
Yes! there you are, so quiet and so stout:
How sly you were to let me find it out!
But I must have one with your autograph—
I mean it—you may spare yourself that laugh.
You'll grace the Council-chamber down below,
And get a sort of Daguerreotypish glow.
We have some specimens of Heliography,
Though yours will be the first one in Photography,
Which I will print, some day, with your Biography.

See! there 'tis written, 'Please to walk up stairs:'
And therefore he who for politeness cares
Can do no less. So, follow me, my friend;
We'll to the Photographic rooms ascend."

4.

Photographists and popular Physicians
Can fill their houses without free admissions:
Thousands, who neither have disease nor phthisic,
Have faith, and gladly pay a fee for physic.
The ugliest mortals do not grudge a ransom
To see their faces, *not* their *souls*, look handsome.
The more like Winterhalter they can flatter,
The greater chance have Artists to grow fatter;
For human vanity won't own the trick,
Though painters lay on beauties an inch thick:
The Portrait speaks more falsely than the Glass,
In which, reflected, man beholds an Ass.

5.

"I want a copy of John Bright, an' please ye,"
Said Hudibras, in manner free and easy;
"I think the likeness good."
"So, Sir, 'tis thought,"
Quoth he from whom the Photograph was bought.
"If you would look at those that hang around,
Some face you know, perhaps, may there be found."
With eager glances, and a flush of pride,
That startled the young stripling by his side,
Said Hudibras, "Yes, yes, I know them all,
Gentle and simple ones, great ones and small!"
Then whispered he to John, and made a sign,
"The *Copies they* may keep, the *Originals* are *mine!*"

6.

Sitting in one of those peculiar chairs,
In that manipulating room up stairs,
Which, like all charming garrets next the sky,
Is always very airy, very dry,
Where artists of the *high* art always fly,
Behold the Master Spirit of the age!
His left hand resting on an open page,
The right his large and finely chisel'd head
Supporting—about which there may be said
A word or two, in praise of its great beauty—
To write the truth is an Historian's duty.

7.

A lofty brow, as polish'd marble fair,
O'er which, thick clustering, fell his raven hair;

Eyes that like meteors shone, whose ev'ry glance
Had spell-like pow'r to rivet, to entrance;
At one time flashing as with sparks of fire;
Another, beaming with a soft desire:
A mouth not over large, nor sensual quite,
That show'd in gladness teeth of pearly white;
But if some deadly purpose reign'd within,
Revealed a fiendish, cold, sardonic grin;
Each lip, till that dark deed and end were gained,
Firm and unflinching, as a vice, remained.
The long, straight nose, just broad'ning tow'rd the eyes,
A chin where Cupid's dimpled valley lies,
A throat, like Jove's, capacious, fine, and round,
Producing vast variety of sound;
Sometimes, like thunder, scaring man and brute;
Sometimes as sweet as Lover's gentle lute:
His form, so God-like, and of towering height,
Like some proud eagle seemed, prepared for flight.

8.

That's our description; though you snub and quiz it,
I doubt if Mayall, in his Carte de visite,
Will bear me out, or even make so much of him:
It's my opinion that he'll make a smutch of him.
I've sat to him, the Watkinses, and others;
But whether meant for me or for my brothers
'Twere hard to say, since both have long been dead;
But this I know, that neither hair nor head
Are mine: the first is woolly like a Nigger;
The second, like a Brigand, though much bigger.
And then for my complexion, which is fair,
No Ethiop ever was so dark, I swear.

Quite inadvertently my hands they put in it;
That is, the clever Artist put his foot in it.
I've suffered martyrdom in ev'ry guise,
Have got in Camera conflicts two black eyes;
My light moustache looks like a blacking brush,
Each line a gutter down which waters rush.
I have not got a favorite wart, nor pimple,
Though at my chin-point, truly, there's a dimple:
What have I done, that this, admired by women,
Is made a well-hole, deep enough to swim in?
Poor Hudibras! I really pity you,
If you but go through half that *I've* gone through.

9.

'Twas like—that's all that we can say for it—
So like, he did not hesitate to pay for it;
But such enquiring look fell from friend Schiller,
When he surveyed the sovereign and the siller,
That it may be worth while to ask the question,
What was it that so ruffled his digestion?
When first he placed the forceps to his head, he
Did this, as they all do, to keep him steady,
The Artist pass'd his fingers through the locks
Of that stern sitter, sitting in the stocks—
Or rather call it sitting upon thorns—
And found two lumps, or bumps, that had been horns.
A kind of shivering ague o'er him came,
Just like an aspen trembled his whole frame;
He shook so much, that, to some people's thinking,
He had the palsy, or he had been drinking.
But neither was the case; 'twas the reverse;
And when the Artist saw him take his purse

And pay, and bow politely at the door,
He inwardly expressed, " my fears are o'er;
But I, Sir, never wish to see you more!"

10.

" You ne'er beheld a race-course, I dare say,"
Cried Hudibras, as sauntering on their way.
" Never," quoth John; " I Racers hate, and Races;
I loathe such people, and shun all such places."

" But I have ordered out our trim balloon,
And, ' coute qui coute,' John, you shall see one soon.
The Doncaster St. Leger will be run there,
And thousands upon thousands lost and won there!
So, take your Mappin razor and some soap,
And, like the Poet Campbell, live on hope.
'Tis four o'clock—the weather very fine—
And we can just blow down in time to dine.
The Preacher says, ' man's life is full of sorrow'!
Let him come down to us this time to-morrow."

11.

There's fascination in a tone of voice
Which makes the listener's heart leap and rejoice;
Some of those big-wigged Barristers oft try it,
Bewitch the Jury, and their cause gain by it.
'Tis wrong, perhaps, mere eloquence should thrive,
Persuading fools that two and two make five;
But human nature's piggish and perverse;
If things are bad, it likes to make them worse.
The passions, not the judgment, are the mark;
Reason they hoodwink, keep her in the dark:

So, between wife and husband, tears prevail,
When truth and justice have been known to fail.

12.

One may roam England through, and never meet
A town like Doncaster, so clean, so sweet.
I have a weakness for the dear, old place,
As many of life's early scenes I trace,
Scenes that the youthful mind long treasures,
Glowing with hopes, affections, pleasures,
Pure and unsullied as the morning's beam
That plays upon the clear, unruffled stream.

On yon green course we marched, in gay parade,
With colours flying, as the music played;
I but a youth in a militia corps—
A Sub.—a poor Lieutenant—nothing more.
There was no fighting, for the war was over;
Duty was pleasant, and we lived in clover.
But Love, who rules in peace or war the same,
Pursued his wonted, unrelenting game,
And quickly set my bosom in a flame.
If I had not loved music, and liked verses,
Likings that may be comforts, or prove curses,
I had not penn'd an Ode unto the Moon,
Nor ventured London Cynics to lampoon.
All have beginnings; by some strange prognostic,
My first essay in rhyme was an Acrostic.

13.

" Well, here we are, John, safely in the Stand,"
Quoth Hudibras; " they rightly call it Grand:

It is a sight worth seeing, you'll agree,
Which in no other country you can see.

Look on those lovely women! those dear creatures,
With such high bonnets and such handsome features!
And then, those high-bred men! all Autocrats,
If one may judge by their cravats, or hats."

" For aught we know," said John, with quiet air,
" The greatest Black-legs may be standing there.
Your well-dress'd blackguards always pick good places
At Bible-meetings mostly,—and the Races.
Near those who horses train, or bet, or ride,
It is not safe to sit, nor stand beside.
If they would drug or poison a fine horse
For money, they would murder us of course."

14.

It was a glorious day! fine autumn weather!
A right good start; they all kept well together,
Till, reaching the red house, some fell away,
And four or five crack jockeys made good play.
There was immense excitement in the scene;
Scarlet was back'd, and two to one on green;
Both favorites; 'twas the toss up of a pin
Which of the twain would have the luck to win.
When yellow, who had kept some lengths behind,
Made desperate strides, and, flying like the wind,
Came neck and neck with his two fellow riders,
Which raised a shout of joy from the outsiders.
Just at the winning post, green tripp'd and fell;
Then rose a fearful cry, a perfect yell.

Scarlet was seen to lurch and lose his place,
As yellow made a dash and won the race

15.

What a sensation! what a fuss! what trouble!
Some had lost fortunes, some increasd them double.
Ladies—sweet, sporting Ladies! meek as Doves!
Had gained a dozen Kids—or more—of Gloves.
Many a Sweep, around that race-course hov'rin',
Had got the Field and pocketed a Sov'reign.
Things a sad turn unluckily had taken,
The Scarlet Runner could not save his bacon.
And some looked *very* green when they beheld
The cause that to the ground their hopes had fell'd.
The yellow dwarf, with winning art most pliant,
Had put to rout full many a gambling Giant;
Some were defaulters, some made up their books;
Some were true Pawns, some look'd most thoro' Rooks.
The faces of J. B. and Hudibras that minute
Said, "thank the stars! *we* have risk'd nothing in it."

16.

As they descended, voices were heard jangling;
Two, Gentlemen of course, were fighting, wrangling:
"You are a Swindler, Sir!" the fair man cried;
"Your whiskers, eye-brows, and moustache are dy'd.
You're some impostor, I'll be bound to say,
To lose a thousand without means to pay."

"Sare," said the Foreigner that seemed to be,
"Vat satisfaction do you vant from me?

I bet—de horse I back'd—he did not vin—
Dat vas no fault of mine—dat is no sin—
I have no money—how can I requite you?
If you are not contented, I vill fight you!"

"Duck him!" some cried; "here is a pond hard by."
"Duck him indeed! I'd like to see you try!"
A dark-eyed damsel said, raising her veil.
The sight made John and Hudibras turn pale;
For, in that fashionable trim, stood there
The Heroine at Verrey's and St. James's Square.

17.

There was a momentary lull—all wondered;
So have we seen a calm before it thundered.
The fair, ill-treated gentleman had been
To bring some active fellows to the scene,
On whom he could rely to aid his plan.
They collared him—that very self-same man—
Despite the little antics of his watchful wife,
Who swore she would defend him with her life;
He was her husband, a real Count by birth,
The dearest, meekest creature on God's earth!
As she was going further to explain,
One of the followers of Sir Richard Mayne
Stept in, and, guided by the Hue and Cry,
Had set his mark on that dark Count just by,
Who met, with fear and trembling, that Policeman's
eye.

18.

"You are my prisoner! I to jail commit you!
Try on these Darbies; I dare say they'll fit you."

" For vat ?" the Count roared out.
" Enquire no further !
'Tis a small case of Forgery and Murder."
" Forgery and Murder ! " cried the wife, distress'd.
" Forgery and Murder ! " echoed all the rest.
Quoth Hudibras, as he arranged his cape,
" Why, John, we've had a very near escape.
That woman might have led *you* on to sin:
You see what scrape she's got that fellow in.
Come back to London ; for, though bad the place is,
You're safer there than staying at the Races."

19.

" That's a good sample of your betting Genus !
'Twas well," said John, " he did not stand between us ;
Our purses would have soon chang'd hands, no doubt.
They've got him safe—I hope they'll serve him out.
We have too many of that stamp at large ;
He'll travel free, soon, at the country's charge ;
And when within a convict's cell he lies,
I hope they'll keep him there until he dies.
Your punishment remitting rules
Are but the Logic of a pack of fools ;
The penitence of murderers and house-breakers
Is much like sorrow shown by undertakers,
Who, in their hearts, are downright glad and merry,
And drink safe voyage to the souls they ferry."

20.

" You're right ! Philanthropy is thrown away.
I love," cried Hudibras, " despotic sway :

No compromising with your arrant thief;
Preach as you will, he has but one belief—
'Tis virtue to defraud his fellow man,
And he *will* rob him always when he can.
Those malefactors, who begin to grieve
And wipe a few sham tears off with their sleeve,
Obtain, at last, a Ticket, not for soup, but leave
To murder, with encouragement to thieve.

The bumps of vice that on men's sculls are found
Are like so many seeds sown in the ground,
That will spring up in spite of each endeavour
To keep them down. Propensities endure for ever;
At least, so long as man has mortal breath;
Then comes, at last, 'the ruling passion strong in death'."

21.

"I knew," said John, "once, an Australian friend
Who thought the worst of Convicts he could mend;
He had those womanly ideas, sheer weakness,
Which saintly-minded folks term meekness,
And placed his only child, a grown-up daughter,
With one of the convicted gang, who music taught her.
This fellow had a forgery committed,
And as the 'Felon Gentleman' was twitted.
My well-intentioned friend would argue still
His Christian plan to turn the evil will
Into a righteous course—change bad to good—
The Tiger wean from its strong love for blood;
The fierce Hyena to a Fawn transform;
Arrest the whirl-wind, or subdue the storm.

Vain hope! that fiend had eaten of the fruit
Whose source was poisoned at the very root;
He lived debased, degraded, and defiled,
Deceived the father, and destroyed his child."

22.

"And yet such serpents are let loose, set free,"
Quoth Hudibras, "again upon society?
'Tis a reproach to English Legislation!
An everlasting blot upon the nation.
It shows how lost to ev'ry sense of shame
The culprits, too, must be whom they'd reclaim.
One would have thought that, after their disgrace,
They would not like to look on an old face,
Nor wish to greet a friend nor comrade more;
Who, not from mere misfortune, shuts the door
Against them, but for some foul, heinous crime
That cannot be wiped out by tears nor time."

23.

"It is not very long since," John replied,
"That one of these Botanic-Bay-trees tried
To graft a shoot into some noble sprigs,
And get presented among Courtly Whigs.
He did so manage as, by hook or crook,
To twine his boughs around a noble Duke,
And at the Drawing Room of our good Queen
This powdered Convict, cap and sword, was seen.
He formerly had been a kind of Lawyer,
But never what was reckoned a Top-sawyer;
Yet, forging Bonds and Bills, and Wills, is easy,
If you but make the road you travel greasy;

And get your hand well into some one's pocket,
Who will entrust you with a Deed or Docket.
What pow'r in a black coat and white cravat!
Waiters and undertakers study that.
This worthy got up the white choker well;
It acted on his clients like a spell.
Old Ladies, whose Bank Dividends he drew
To save them trouble, quite enjoyed to view
The meek Attorney in his sable suit,
His high, starched collar, and cravat to boot;
And said, with smile that was almost hysterical,
" He's such a charming man! he looks so clerical!"

24.

" I've no doubt, John, but that this chap had gold.
He knew well *that* in England's a sure hold.
If he were likewise impudent and bold,
He might have company in vast variety,
And get into the very best society.
Your Nuggets are the Nucleus for all,
On money'd men the proudest Prince will call.
Who has forgotten when the Railroad King
A swarm of Nobles and Grandees could bring
Around him, like a swarm of Bees? The Honey
He had hived up in that large house was money;
And *that* the world will worship more than worth,
Or all the talent that e'er shone on earth:
There is no reputation, howe'er rotten,
But will be sound, if money can be gotten.

25.

" Considering, John, how heavily you're tax'd
To thieves transport, Laws need not be relax'd

To bring them back. Let your Policemen glance
At those who follow out *their* trade in France,
And mark the difference. Here, beneath their noses,
Crime, in a thousand shapes and forms, reposes.
While letter A his nightly round is blinking,
And Polly's Master's double X is drinking,
Swearing he loves her better far than beer,
Some Miscreant is committing murder near,
Cuts a poor Needle-woman's throat, and gets off clear.
But if, at midnight, just before 'tis morn,
A few young Guards, not Black-guards, at Cremorne,
Are over-charged with Gooseberry Champagne,
Or punch a head or two ' à la romaine,"
The vigilance of letter A is past belief;
He treats a Gentleman more like a thief,
Uses his truncheon from no provocation,
And carries off the Guardsman to the Station;
And when the hearing comes, then letter A
Will swear that he was struck in the affray,
And bring another letter—letter B—
To swear to really what he did *not* see—
A case of downright, wilful perjury.
The Gentleman is guilty; A and B outshine him:
How *could* a Magistrate do less than fine him?

26.

" I'll take you to a place, *prove* what I say,
That crime's notorious in the light of day.
The Round House in St. Giles's is just by,
Where girls and boys their thievish calling ply.
You see those ragged urchins at the back,
Tossing and pitching? Hark! one cries out ' black!'

He signals a Policeman's on the beat:
They're quiet till he makes a sure retreat.
Those Imps, small though they seem, would fob you,
And, if alone, would knock you down and rob you.
They tore an old man's eyes out of their sockets,
And after taking all from both his pockets,
Which was but four-pence, cudgell'd him, and curs'd [him,
Then led him forth, as if they'd fed and nurs'd him.
Yon girls, that you discover in low dresses,
Are not mere wantons, seeking for caresses;
Plunder's their game; with cunning art they try
To coax you, as the spider did the fly,
Into their room; then they profess to like you,
And pat you gently on the cheek, *not* strike you,
And by degrees secure your watch and studs,
Your hat and boots, and other worldly goods;
Then, not unmindful of what they're about,
Unlock the door, and turn you naked out.

27.

" There's my old friend, T. Grieve, time-honor'd name!
The King of Artists! First of Scenic fame!
Surrounded by these fiends, whose foul breath taints
The air of that old chapel where he paints;
His life's not worth a straw, if once these Elves
E'er take a fancy to the paint themselves;
Though it would bring them all to shame and dolor,
Did they lay hands but on that man of color.
Why, stunning Joe, who once the Rookery kept,
Where Criminals of all sorts ate and slept,
Would ne'er have sanctioned any of his thieves
To hurt a hair of that paint-brush of Grieve's.

" But custom seems to justify abuses,
Or else our large police force of no use is.
There's not a day that one may not behold
Low, dirty, half-clothed Children, hungry, cold,
Lying about the streets, the pictures of despair.
Why is it so? They should be some one's care.
Whose duty is it to enquire, find out
Whether they be in want, or only tout
For pence to keep some squalid wretch in gin,
The Mother of that child of Misery and Sin?

28.

Turn we, awhile, from graver scene to gay:
The eager crowd is thronging on its way,
St. James's and Pall Mall are filled with faces
All dressed in smiles, to see the Courtly Graces,
Lounging along, half languishing, half lazy,
In coaches—some with coronets, some crazy—
Of all degrees of beauty, of all ages,
Looking like Birds of Paradise in cages.
One need not wonder, huddled so together,
If, now and then, their tails should lose a feather;
And yet, at Drawing Rooms, and at a marriage,
How much is stowed away in one poor carriage!

29.

Now they are on the move—if it be slow,
It *is* a move—the tide begins to flow;
The Club Disciples lay their papers by,
To catch a glance from some fair Courtier's eye.
" You see that Blonde?" cried Scroggles to Sir Harry;
" That's the young Lady Julia Irish Tim's to marry.

A rosy-cheeked, good-tempered looking girl,
Rolling in wealth, the daughter of an Earl,
In these hard times is not so bad a catch:
I should not grieve myself at such a match.
A fortune and a pleasant physiognomy
Might reconcile one to the Home Economy."

30.

"But I have heard," said Harry, "Lady *Juliar*,
As Cockneys call her, is a girl peculiar;
Rides over flood and fell—at steeple chases—
Follows the hounds—bets deeply at the races—
Has boxing gloves and foils hung round the room,
And smokes and drinks like some low, stable groom."
"She'll not alarm the native modesty of Tim,"
Cried Scroggles; "all the virtues dwell in him.
'Tis true he's half a Papist, and loves play,
And runs in debt with no intent to pay;
And though his Sire's allowance is but scant,
He spends that little on a Figurante. [pagne,
Save love of Cards and Dice, Prize-fighting, and Cham-
Tim's not so bad a fellow in the *main*.
I cannot say his learning is profuse;
'Bell's Life,' and 'Ulcerated London News,'
Make up the sum and substance of his reading.
Wisdom's a stumbling-block to men of breeding;
And Cards and Dice must first have been invented
For those whose *minds*, not *morals*, were tormented.
Those painted, pasteboard Kings and Queens, and
Have hurried thousands to untimely graves. [Knaves,
Those dented bits of bone, could they declare,
Would tell sad tales of ruin and despair.
Your Gamester murder plots o'er his pork-chop,
And winds his course up with the usual *Drop*.

31.

The Pageant's over, with its Regal State,
And Penances that on all Court Days wait;
Trumpets are sounding, Royalty is moving,
And loyal Subjects, dutiful and loving,
Along the lines in countless numbers seen,
Are pealing forth "Huzzah!" "God bless the Queen!"
Weary, and worn out with the heat and crush,
Dames who have been presented homeward rush.
The Country Squire and his five chubby daughters
Have seen the *real* Britannia of the Waters,
And letters from the post will fly by dozens
To tell the fact to all their loving Cousins.
'Tis marvellous how women like to write,
When they've a chance, and matter to indite.
I had an Aunt whose tongue could cut and thrust
Like any sword—it ne'er was known to rust,
'Twas in such daily use—and yet, her pen
Was quite as fluent—she was feared by men.
To find a Beetle in Aunt Deborah's boots
Would bring an essay on what she calls "brutes,"
Proving their instincts, appetites, and habits.
She had aversions—hated rats and rabbits;
But I have known her fill eight sheets of post
About the difference 'twixt a boil and roast.
She had her sins and follies, like her betters;
But these we hope are buried—with her letters.

32.

Turn we, awhile, from gayer scene to grave:
The Sun has set that life and lustre gave
To all around in busy street and park;
The night is cold and heavy, damp and dark;

Slow and incessant falls the chilling rain
On scores of homeless poor, who hope to gain
Within yon workhouse respite from their woes,
For one sad night, find victuals and repose.
See! the door opens, the Official eyes
The shivering wretches with no marked surprise;
It is no novel scene to waken fears,
He is accustomed to their rags and tears;
He but surveys that squalid group with care,
To know if any hapless being standing there
Has shared before the bounty of the Board.
If so, he must refuse; they can't afford
To make a refuge of their Casual Ward;
'Tis not the custom, Guardian Laws are hard.
But half of those in miserable plight
Find food and housing for a single night;
True outcasts are the rest, shut out, forlorn,
They well may wish they never had been born:
Life is no boon to them; their aching bones
Revive not, lying on the cold, wet stones.

33.

There should be no such harrowing scenes as these
In England, with its wealth and luxuries.
Shelter, though rugged,—food, though coarse it be,
Belongs to each class of humanity.
It may be they are dissolute and base,
A low, demoralized, degraded race:
Yet indolence and recklessness we trace
In upper ranks, where spendthrift sons become
A burden to their relatives at home,
Who, were their vices not with favour met,

Might such reception at Saint Martin's get,
Some night when they were hungry, cold and wet.

34.

"Why is good Jacob Omnium's pen cut short
That drove the Thieves from out the Palace Court?
There never was a place so foul, so rank;
The very threshold with corruption stank:
The Judge, the Jury, Lawyers, Beadle, Crier,
Should, years before, have been consumed by fire;
Nor one polluted stone upon another left,
To mark the scene of so much wrong and theft.
How many ruined Tradesmen had good need
To curse the Laws that made their hearts to bleed.
And yet, John, with your Commons and your Peers,
This Den of Infamy had life for years;
And I have heard, which you would blush to mention,
The Government gave ev'ry Rogue a Pension.

35.

The snow falls lightly, it wants long to day,
The noise of many hammers dies away;
The scaffold is prepared, a tragedy to play.
Thousands of heartless, haggard, grimy scamps,
A surging sea of Thieves, of Roughs and Tramps,
Shouting and shivering in the wintry air,
Are densely pack'd, like Hounds in one vast Lair,
To witness Ketch arrange the fatal tie—
Five Pirates from Manilla are to die.
They had done murder on the lonely deep,
Had stol'n upon the Captain in his sleep,
And butcher'd others in cool blood, on board
"The Flow'ry Land," a merchant vessel, stor'd

With wines for Cargo, bound to Singapore;
The Crew, the lowest type, about a score
Of Spaniards, Germans, Greeks, and other nations,
Ruffians who asked no blessing with their rations.

36.

To *comfortably* view those wretched Pirates
Swing on the Gallows, rooms at very high rates
Are let to Guardsmen, Great Grandees and Doxies,
By "Touters," at the price of Grand Tier Boxes:
There be those who would pay the sum they ask,
Whose morbid appetites delight to bask
On Hangmen's Caps or Ballet Girls in Spangles:
Who, while the Gibbet-fruit before them dangles,
Shout,'midst a show'r of groans and taunts, and hisses,
"O! what an edifying lesson this is!
Let us improve the scene on which we dwell,
And drink Morality in this Moselle!"

37.

A Foreign, *not* a Heaven-born, Minister—
It was indecent, if not sinister —
Applied by letter to an Alderman:
In some such strain as this the billet ran:

"Dear Sir,
A mutual friend, who loves a sight,
Wishes to sleep in Newgate for one night,
To view the Execution done on Monday;—
If you could make arrangements for next Sunday
To put him up, not *tuck* him up, 'twould be
A favour, worthy Sir, conferred on me."
In some respects—'tis wonder to relate—
The Cit refused the Minister of State.
The disappointed friend went home instead,
And ate a Lobster before going to bed;

Forgetting Banting's night-cap, "that's the question;"
Of course he had a fit of indigestion,
And pass'd a restless night, nor slept a wink,
Till day-light through the curtains 'gan to blink;
Then he had fearful struggles, loudly scream'd,—
The fact was that he did not sleep, but dream'd
Five swarthy Corses floated in the air,
Divested of those Caps poor wretches wear
When they're turned off,—it was the lack of Banting,
The *Spiritual* Night-cap that was wanting
To lay the body of that crusty Lobster,
One else had heard no groan, nor seen his Nob stir,
As starting to his feet, still breathing quick,
He bellow'd "bravo, Ketch! you've done the trick."

38.

Outside the crowd of Riff-Raff without qualms,
Strange, lantern-visag'd objects, chanting psalms
And bearing Flags religiously inscribed,
The mob exhorted, who but jeer'd and gibed
At those lean, canting Maw-worms them haranguing,
And cried, "Oh! tis a glorious sight, a hanging!"
Then to the Tavern, swarming like a hive,
These "Roughs" repair to keep the game alive.

39.

The Law is satisfied—Mosaic Law,
That governs Christians, deems it just to draw
Another's blood for every drop that 's shed.
It may be wisdom, Sages so have said:
But that all-wise, omniscient, perfect Being,
Whose eye is ever watchful and all-seeing,
Of provocation and ill-usage judges,
And sums up worldly-fashion'd human grudges,

Weighs in a nicer balance than we show
The fiery passions that within us glow;
Traces the cause that goads us on to ill,
Shows mercy where frail mortals blood would spill;
He knows if those five Mariners were wrong'd,
If they'd been spurn'd, like dogs, kick'd, cuff'd and
thong'd.
Foul water, insufficient food, and blows,
For service render'd, would turn friends to foes,
A sense of injury they would retain,
Till the rous'd blood grew curdled in each vein;
And murd'rous steel would stain the hand of man,
If once a reign of Tyranny began.
Is Justice even-handed? Do the rich
With poorer criminals fall in the ditch?
Or, if they fall from high to low estate,
Will not some well-paid Counsel on them wait,
Some ready, skilful Quibbler be at hand
To drag the Culprit quietly to land,
And, while the ground seems trembling 'neath his feet,
Securely lodge him in some safe retreat,
Defraud the Hangman and the Law defeat?

40.

Why did not Townley flutter in the breeze,
Like those five dusky Pirates of the Seas?
His crime exceeded theirs, though the Home Sec.
Might deem him guiltless, pure without a speck;
He had his senses, was as keen and quick
As an Incendiary who fires a Rick,
Or some Promoter of Joint Stocks or Schemes—
His mind was wakeful even in his dreams;

He had, besides, some very good connexions;
I wish him joy of them, and *his* reflections!
In Copy Books with virtuous lines they cram us,
" Evil Companions must corrupt and damn us,"
Yet having good connexions is no reason
Why Justice should be hobbling out of season.

41.

Boileau once said, the " World is full of Fools;"
So there is plenty work yet for the Schools;
If Murderers and Maniacs be the same,
We hazard much in life's eventful game,
And every man, if one there be with sense,
Should carry a revolver for defence;
For these mad people are so precious cunning,
They'd stab you in the very act of funning,
As would-be wits garrôte you with their punning.

42.

Hark! from Whitehall to Charing Cross, a shout!
Assembled thousands keep a sharp look out:
For hours have dirty boys on Charles's statue
Been chaffing all around and staring at you,
Maiming the martyr in both hands and feet:
Atrocious Urchins! but revenge is sweet.
Some day the stony King will downward come,
And reckoning take for loss of toe and thumb;
The monarch's thirst for vengeance might be 'sated,
At being cruelly decapitated,
If some poor Devil's neck were dislocated.
Hark! louder still they shout "he comes! he comes!"
The trumpets clamour, gaily roll the drums,

Hats, Handkerchiefs are waving to and fro,
Wonder and Expectation on tip-toe;
Eyeballs that have been sorely strain'd and tax'd,
Within their sockets feel reliev'd, relax'd;
Before the crowd of gazers stands a Hero,
No sanguinary Tyrant, such as Nero.
Giuseppe Garibaldi, gen'rous, brave, alert,
A warm heart beats beneath that scarlet shirt.
There may be many of those standing by,
Joining in that glad, universal cry,
Who only know the General by name;
Who have not mark'd the Soldier's course to fame.
Suppose we bring some leading scenes before us,
And act Macbeth *without* the Witches' Chorus,
Revealing, as in Banquo's magic mirror,
A Line of Glories with no single error.

43.

Twice, while his youthful lip was only downing,
He swam and sav'd two fellow men from drowning;
Then, like our own sweet Bird, Miss Nightingale,
Where suff'rers lay in Hospital and Jail,
Dying of Cholera at Marseilles, he kept
A constant vigil, seldom ate or slept;
The Peasants viewed him as an angel pure,
The Priests, good Catholics, "a perfect Cure!"
Behold him next, in a far worse condition,
Thumb-screw'd and tortured by the Inquisition;
On every side "Familiar Faces" grin,
And hope Confession from his lips to win;
But that would compromise—a Friend betray,
So the brave Lion keeps the Hounds at Bay—
A look defiant only on them throws,
And scorns to yield to his tormenting foes.

Chance gives the Leader of these hated Bands,
Another time, into Giuseppe's hands,
Who, heedless of the wrong this fiend had wrought him,
Does not, as many would when they had caught him,
Suspend him from the nearest tow'r or tree,
But nobly grants him Life and Liberty.
Virtue most rare! such Charity 's confounding,
And seems of Justice but a strange compounding;
We argu'd somewhat diff'rently in youth,
"For ev'ry Eye an Eye, for ev'ry Tooth a Tooth."

44.

What brings the Patriot to this Land of Wealth?
He needs repose, he comes in search of health:
A noble Duke, with views of large expansion,
Has offer'd him the run of his fine mansion,
All that can sate the eye, or charm the ear,
Viands to stimulate, choice wines to cheer,
In vast profusion sore temptations offer;
Yet, hermit like, he shuns the joys they proffer:
For all who would not to the fact be blinded
Know that the General is but simple-minded,
A very Anchorite, a Sage, none wiser,
An early Rooster and an early Riser.

45.

Time journeys on—the lordly and the lowly,
The City Chamberlain and Mr. Bowley,
F. Gye and others who in turtle trade
Have gained some glory—query? money made—
By this good, kind and honest-hearted man;
Money 's the cry, make Money while you can,
For Testimonial or some special Fund,
No matter which, let all the World be dunn'd.

One cannot see a real, live Hero ev'ry day,
And curious folks for peeping ought to pay.
We Covent Garden should "Bear Garden" call
On that renownèd night at Floral Hall,
Where City Aldermen with their fat Wives,
Gold-chained and crinolined as for their lives,
So elbowed, jostled him at every step he
Took, that the tender ribs of poor Giuseppe
Ran risk of being fairly broken in,
Perhaps they trod, too, on his wounded shin.
With struggles for hand-shaking and caresses,
Some Dames had need of darning up their dresses;
While many a frontlet and disordered Wig
Provok'd the mirth of each young Opera Sprig,
Whose Seat 's a Stall, whose Entry Card a Bone is,
Himself, at least, Apollo or Adonis.

46.

Time journeys on—these fètes and City dining
Occasion, in High Places, some repining;
The Hero cannot eat all set before him,
He cannot visit all who now implore him;
He grows, they cry, too popular by half,
And will not bow down to the Golden Calf,
Refuses, tho' it may seem rather funny,
The Garibaldian Fund of Sterling Money,
Rais'd to provide him with a new Estate,
And Luxuries fit for any Potentate;
He covets no Domain with new Devices,
Caprera's ample, for each want suffices:
Corn, Wine and Oil, with flesh and milk of Goats,
Are quite as good as Bank of England Notes
To him whose habits are so pure and simple
As ne'er to raise upon his skin a single pimple.

47.

We could remind these Working Men's Committees,
Who chaunt the "Inno Garibaldi" ditties,
He might refuse Estates and such like trifles,
But *not* decline a million English Rifles.
These active Delegates of Country Traders,
Collecting moneys to assist Invaders,
Had better to their Lasts and Shop-boards stick
Than aid a measure so impolitic;
To conquer Naples and her Lazzaroni
Was easy as to swallow Maccaroni;
Between their Laziness and Impotence,
Such coward, dastard Knaves, make no defence,
Were Neapolitans e'er shown to be
Deserving of a name in Chivalry?
They basely left poor Pepè in the muck,
And lost their freedom from the want of Pluck;
The King who rules o'er that disgraceful set
From them can neither love nor honour get,
No Conquest, then, for Garibaldi claim,
For beating Men unworthy of the name.

48.

Should he prove rash enough to leave his home
To oust the reigning Pope, dismember Rome,
Or rush on Venice with a madman's ire,
He'll fairly put his fingers in the fire;
The French and Austrians only "bide their time"
To check this march of Freedom—call it crime—
Venice belongs to Austria, 'tis her right,
For which she now prepares and means to fight;
France must the ancient Catholic Creed defend,
Assistance to good Pio Nono lend.

Our Bishops we might just as well decry,
As temporal Pow'r unto the Pope deny;
'Tis doubtful if the Vatican's Arm Chair
Bear half the weight that Wolsey's used to bear.
Our Cardinal's expensive ways might spring
From fancying he was *greater* than the King;
But Italy's anointed Roman Head
Is sparing in its Oil, its Wine, its Bread;
He has few Vices, few Extravagancies,
Few costly Sins engender'd by Romances;
Let all well-wishers to Giuseppe hope
He may escape the Rapier and the Rope:
But, then, he must not meddle with the Pope.

49.

"A Telegram! I'm wanted, John; good bye!
I cannot govern well by Deputy.
We have some sad rebellious knaves below,
Who only wait the word to strike a blow:
My longer absence might advantage give;
But I will rule as long as e'er I live.
To be your friend I have sincerely striven;
So profit by the hints that I have given.
There's much that you may learn from 'la belle France,'
Besides the minuet and way to dance.
Don't let her mix you up with any quarrels;
You'll only have to pay, and get no laurels.
That last affair with Russia was unwise;
All other ships but yours the Czar defies.
And don't about those Polanders go fight;
If Russia's wrong, let others set her right.

But you might lend a hand to those brave Danes,
And get some thanks from Europe for your pains;
Those big Boys fighting such a little Chap,
Is something more than merely a mishap;
Let all this Conference and Burlesquing end,
'Tis time that England should prove Denmark's friend,
Despite Diplomacy in Downing Street, be sure
Prevention is a wiser course than Cure;
This Schleswig Question had not come to blood,
If matters had been rightly understood;
Let 's hope that Right will triumph over Might,
So, till again we meet, old Friend, good night!"

FINIS.

J. MALLETT, PRINTER, WARDOUR STREET, SOHO, LONDON.

www.ingramcontent.com/pod-product-compliance
Lightning Source LLC
Chambersburg PA
CBHW020255090426
42735CB00009B/1095

* 9 7 8 3 7 4 4 7 1 3 1 1 5 *